The Court Secret by James Shirley

A TRAGI-COMEDY. Never Acted, But prepared for the Scene at Black Friers.

James Shirley was born in London in September 1596.

His education was through a collection of England's finest establishments: Merchant Taylors' School, London, St John's College, Oxford, and St Catharine's College, Cambridge, where he took his B.A. degree in approximately 1618.

He first published in 1618, a poem entitled Echo, or the Unfortunate Lovers.

As with many artists of this period full details of his life and career are not recorded. Sources say that after graduating he became "a minister of God's word in or near St Albans." A conversion to the Catholic faith enabled him to become master of St Albans School from 1623–25.

He wrote his first play, Love Tricks, or the School of Complement, which was licensed on February 10th, 1625. From the given date it would seem he wrote this whilst at St Albans but, after its production, he moved to London and to live in Gray's Inn.

For the next two decades, he would write prolifically and with great quality, across a spectrum of thirty plays; through tragedies and comedies to tragicomedies as well as several books of poetry. Unfortunately, his talents were left to wither when Parliament passed the Puritan edict in 1642, forbidding all stage plays and closing the theatres.

Most of his early plays were performed by Queen Henrietta's Men, the acting company for which Shirley was engaged as house dramatist.

Shirley's sympathies lay with the King in battles with Parliament and he received marks of special favor from the Queen.

He made a bitter attack on William Prynne, who had attacked the stage in Histriomastix, and, when in 1634 a special masque was presented at Whitehall by the gentlemen of the Inns of Court as a practical reply to Prynne, Shirley wrote the text—The Triumph of Peace.

Shirley spent the years 1636 to 1640 in Ireland, under the patronage of the Earl of Kildare. Several of his plays were produced by his friend John Ogilby in Dublin in the first ever constructed Irish theatre; The Werburgh Street Theatre. During his years in Dublin he wrote The Doubtful Heir, The Royal Master, The Constant Maid, and St. Patrick for Ireland.

In his absence from London, Queen Henrietta's Men sold off a dozen of his plays to the stationers, who naturally, enough published them. When Shirley returned to London in 1640, he finished with the Queen Henrietta's company and his final plays in London were acted by the King's Men.

On the outbreak of the English Civil War Shirley served with the Earl of Newcastle. However when the King's fortunes began to decline he returned to London. There his friend Thomas Stanley gave him help and thereafter Shirley supported himself in the main by teaching and publishing some educational works under the Commonwealth. In addition to these he published during the period of dramatic eclipse four small volumes of poems and plays, in 1646, 1653, 1655, and 1659.

It is said that he was "a drudge" for John Ogilby in his translations of Homer's Iliad and the Odyssey, and survived into the reign of Charles II, but, though some of his comedies were revived, his days as a playwright were over.

His death, at age seventy, along with that of his wife, in 1666, is described as one of fright and exposure due to the Great Fire of London which had raged through parts of London from September 2nd to the 5th.

He was buried at St Giles in the Fields, in London, on October 29th, 1666.

Index of Contents

To The Right Honourable William Earl of Strafford, Viscount Wentworth, Baron Wentworth of Wentworth, Woodhouse, Newmarsh, Oversley, and Raby.

My Lord,

The Character of true Nobilitie is sacred, and indeleble; that Yours is such, needeth no Testimony, the World bearing witnesse to Your Honourable Mind, upon which all other accesse of Titles wait like a fair Train of Attendance, not Ornaments, Your own Virtue giving them lustre, and enterteining them as Rewards payd down to Your Person, and Merit.

This Principle, gave me boldnesse to make this approach to Your Lordship, and not without some design in my Ambition, to renew my self to Your smile, who have enjoyed the happinesse (many yeares since) to kisse Your hand, and to observe with Admiration the Beauties that shin'd upon Your Youth, which as they gained upon Time, so they have grown above the prejudice of Opinion, and improv'd their Maturitie by the Earlinesse of their Spring.

But my humble duty (my Lord) at this fortunate hour to attend You, cometh not alone, it bringeth a Present, such as my weak condition could reach to; a Poem, one, that weareth no Ribbands in the forehead; not so much as warranted by Applause; for it happened to receive birth, when the Stage was interdicted, and wanted that publique Seal which other Compositions enjoyed; Though it hath been read and honour'd with the Allowance of some men, whose Opinion was as acceptable to mee, as the Vote of a smiling Theater.

But this is not to prescribe to your Honour, whom I have by this Application made my Iudge (should You wave the Patron) and from whom there lyes no Appeal.

If your Honour, descending from your higher Contemplations, vouchsafe to look upon these Papers, though Your Justice should condemn them, it would bee their Reputation to fall by so Honourable a Sentence: But if they happen to obtain Your Lordships favour, that they may live, your Name will not only be a powerful defence to them, but a lasting Record of Honour upon the Composer, whose heart is full of Devotions to your Lordship, and ambitious of no greater addition, than to be known,

My Lord,
Your most obliged, and humble Servant,
JAMES SHIRLEY,

DRAMATIS PERSONAE
The King of Spain
Roderigo, his Brother
Manuel, the suppos'd son of Piracquo, but the true Carlo, son to the King.
Maria, his Sister
Antonio, Prince of Portugall
Isabella his Sister
Mendoza a Duke
Carlo, suppos'd Prince of Spain, but indeed Julio, the son of Mendoza.
Clara, Mendoza's Daughter
Piracquo, a Nobleman
Two Lords
Pedro, a Kinsman of Piracquo's, Servant to Mendoza
Celio, Page to Carlo
Ladies

Castellano
Messengers
Servants
Guard

Madrid.

ACT I

SCENE I

An Apartment in the Palace.

Enter at one door **DON ANTONIO** leading **MARIA**; at another two **GENTLEMEN**.

1ST GENTLEMAN
The Prince of Portugal, Don Antonio—

2ND GENTLEMAN
He courts our Infanta close.

1ST GENTLEMAN
And may deserve her.

[Enter **DON MANUEL**. **MARIA** lets fall a jewel from her dress, he takes it up, and offers it to her.

MANUEL
Your Grace—

MARIA
'Tis none of mine, Don Manuel.
Will your Highness walk?

[Exit **ANTONIO** & **MARIA**

1ST GENTLEMAN
Observe you that?

2ND GENTLEMAN
The Prince seem'd not well pleas'd.

MANUEL
What doth the Princess mean?
I saw it fall from her.

1ST GENTLEMAN
My eyes are witness,
Noble Don Manuel.

MANUEL
My Lords, your servant.

2ND GENTLEMAN
How do you like the Spanish Court? Although
My Lord your father were a native, yet
Your birth and education were abroad;
Compell'd by your father's destiny.

MANUEL
My unhappiness!
I have heard him say, some policies prevail'd
To make him leave this Kingdom, and his fortunes,
To try his fate at sea, till he found means
To plant himself in Portugal, from whence
He was but late reduc'd by the good Prince,
With promise of a pardon; and his honour
Is full securitie for us.

1ST GENTLEMAN
The Prince
Can do becoming things, and knows good acts
Are in themselves rewards; but the report
Was here, that fifteen thousand Ducats
Were offer'd Roderigo our Kings brother,
By your father Lord Piracquo, to assure
His reconcilement here, for trespasses
He did at sea.

2ND GENTLEMAN
But not accepted.
I know not which will be his more vexation,
To know the Prince's act, restore Piracquo,
Or so much money lost.

[Enter **PRINCE CARLO**, and **CELIO** his Page.

1ST GENTLEMAN
The Prince.

CARLO
Don Manuel,
You are become a man of mighty business,
Or I have lost some interest, I had
Since I left Portugal; but I'll not chide.
Where is the King?

2ND GENTLEMAN
In his Bed chamber, Sir,
With Duke Mendoza.

CARLO
I'll not intterrupt 'em.
You may redeem your error, and we both
Converse again.

[Exit.

MANUEL
You infinitely honor,
And with it bind the obedience of your creature.

1ST GENTLEMAN
Now he is going to his Mistris.

2ND GENTLEMAN [To **CLARA**]
The Duke Mendoza's Daughter.

MANUEL
Mistris? do you forget, my Lord, the treaty,
And his own personall contract, the kiss warm
On Isabella's lip, and strengthned by the hope
And expectation of another Mariage,
Betwixt Anthonio and Maria his Sister?

1ST GENTLEMAN
We are us'd
To freedom here, with as much innocence
I may, perhaps, hereafter say, the Princess
Maria meant you honor, when she dropt
A Jewel; Sir, it cannot be much blemish
For you to own her service.

MANUEL
'T were an insolence
(Beyond her mercy to forgive) in me,
To think she meant it grace, or I apply it

At such a distance of my blood and fortune.
This in a whisper, but convey'd through Court,
Would forfeit me for ever: As y'are honourable,
Preserve me in my humbler thoughts.

1ST GENTLEMAN
Be confident.

2ND GENTLEMAN
And pardon my expression; Sir, your servant.

[Exeunt.

MANUEL
I have observ'd the Princess scatter beams
Upon me, and talk language with her eyes
Sometime, such as I dare not apprehend
With safety, or Religion; for I find
My heart anothers conquest. But the Prince!
Why should he move my jealousie? I know
His amorous thoughts, already plac'd upon
Fair Isabella, must inhabit there,
And meet their just reward; he cannot be
So carelesless of his honour.

[Enter **PEDRO**.

PEDRO
Can you direct me, Sir, to Don Piracquo,
Your noble father? I bring affairs concern him.

MANUEL
You wait upon the Duke Mendoza, Sir?

PEDRO
I was i'th' first number of those attended
His Duchess, while she liv'd; his Grace doth now
Acknowledge me a waiting movable
Within his family; my name is Pedro,
A poor kinsman of yours, if you be, Sir,
My Lord Piracquo's son, and might have been
His heir, had not you Mother been more fruitfull
At sea, before she died, who left you an infant;
'Twas something to my prejudice, but your Father—

MARIA
Is in the privy Garden, Sir.

PEDRO

Your servant.

[Exit.

MARIA

What means this fellow to survay me? ha! Clara!

[Enter **MENDOZA** and **CLARA**.

And her Father Duke Mendoza! I
Must wish a time without his presence, to
Confirm, how much I honour her: Loud fame
Speaks him a noble Gentleman, but of late
(By what misfortune 'tis not known) he hath
Some garbs, that shew not a clear spirit in him.
But that his Lady's dead, men would interpret
His starts proceed from jealousie: I'll leave 'em.
And wait some private opportunity.

[Exit.

CLARA

I must confess, Prince Carlo, Sir, hath courted me,
But with a noble flame.

MENDOZA

Flame me no flame, unless you mean to turn our family
And name to ashes in the Kings displesure.
Thou do'st not know the Prince, as I doe, Clara.

[Enter **PIRACQUO** and **PEDRO**.

PEDRO

Sure you have known me, Sir, I have expected
Some time, when you would own me—

PIRACQUO

Your name's Pedro—

PEDRO

You thought me of your blood, Sir, when you promis'd
I should be your heir; I did a service for't
Deserves your memory, not contempt, my Lord.

PIRACQUO

Oh, thou didst well, and though as I then stood
Proscrib'd, I wisht it otherwise, I now thank

Thy witty cozenage, and allow thy faith
Religious to thy Prince; be honest still.

PEDRO
Honest? you are mistaken, I have been
Honest to none but you, Sir.

PIRACQUO
Be to thy self.

PEDRO
I know not what you mean by witty cozenage;
But to my danger, I may say, I did
The feat as you desir'd; you know I did,
And 'tis my wonder, what we both projected
To make your own conditions for your pardon,
And safe return, after proscription,
Hath not been worth your use so many years;
Where is the Prince?

PIRACQUO
The Prince? you are witty, Kinsman.

PEDRO
Nay if you slight me, Sir, and pay my service
With this neglect, I can undoe my self
To make you find repentance—

[Offers to go.

PIRACQUO
Come nearer—

[They whisper apart.

MENDOZA
Therefore upon my blessing, if thou hast
Such an ambitious thought I charge thee leave it.

CLARA
Sir, you may spare these preeepts, I have not
Given away my freedom, or by promise
Of more than may become my duty, offer'd
The Prince an expectation; I am
Not ignorant he is design'd a Bridegroom
To the fair Isabella, and it were
Sawcie injustice to distract a blessing
Now hovering o'r two Kingdoms—

MENDOZA
Thou art wise;
Preserve this duty. Ha! is not that Pedro?
I doe not like their whisper—

CLARA
You look pale, Sir.

PIRACQUO
Can this be truth? was it Prince Carlo, then
Without imposture was deliver'd me?
Didst thou not couzen me?

PEDRO
If I be mortall, Sir,
It was my Ladies art, for her own safety,
To put this trick upon the Court, which she
Kept me from my Lord, untill upon her death-bed
She made him overseer of the Secret.

MENDOZA [aside]
Did he not name a Secret?

CLARA
You are troubled.

MENDOZA
I? thou art deceiv'd.

PIRACQUO
Ha! 'tis thy Lord Mendoza.

PEDRO
He may take
Some jealousie, if he observe our whisper.

PIRACQUO
Adde, Pedro, but to this, thy future secresie,
Till I mature some act, my thoughts now fix upon,
And choose thy place within my heart; meet me—[Whispers]

PEDRO
Enough, you seal the mystery agen.

MENDOZA
Pedro, come hither; What did you whisper?

[Enter a **GENTLEMAN**.

1ST GENTLEMAN
Duke Roderigo, my Lord, desires
Your conference in the garden.

PIRACQUO
I'll attend him.

[Exeunt with **GENTLEMAN**.

PEDRO
He is my Kinsman, Sir, and did salute me—

MENDOZA
I would thou wert his Cousin ten removes
Pedro, as far as the two Poles are distant.

CLARA
My father need not fear Prince Carlo now;
I find another guest here, 'tis Don Manuel
Holds chief intelligence with my thoughts.

[Exit.

MENDOZA
Well Pedro,
Take heed, my life is in thy lips—

PEDRO
I know my duty, Sir, if you suspect,
Command me to be dumb; Sir, you must trust me.

MENDOZA
I know not how to help it, wait upon
My daughter.

[Exeunt

I would my Lady had liv'd, or died without
Bequeathing me this Legacy on her death-bed,
A Secret to consume me; this servant, whom
I dare not much displease, is all the witness
Survives, sworn with the rest to secresie,
And though I have small argument to suspect him,
After so long a silence, yet I am
Not safe to be at his devotion:
I could soon purge him with a Fig, but that's

Not honest: Was it ever known, a man
So innocent, should have so many Agues
In's conscience? I am weary of the Court;
I must have some device—

[Enter **RODERIGO** with **PIRACQUO**.

Duke Roderigo,
And Don Piracquo? they are whispering too;
This jealousie will take my brains apieces.

[Exit.

RODERIGO
I have said, & now expect, my Lord, your answer.

PIRACQUO
I must acknowledge from your Grace, a favour,
That you have been so clear, and free with me;
I might have thought my self secure i'th' dark,
And ignorant of this expectation,
Incurr'd your Graces jealousie.

RODERIGO
I had allwaies
A firm opinion of your Lordships gratitude.

PIRACQUO
But for the sum, he fifty thousand Ducats,
I must acknowledge, if your Grace had mediated
My pardon then with the good King, your brother,
It had oblig'd my payment; but my cause
Not worth your Graces agitation,
Or breath, was like a vessell struck upon
Some shelf, without all hope t' have say I'd agen,
Had not the Prince's mercie, when he came
To Portugal, reliev'd it with a gale,
And set my bark afloat.

RODERIGO
The Prince?
Why? doth your Lordship think I had no part
I'th' work of your repair? the power, and office
I hold at Court, is not asleep, my Lord,
When any act of grace is done by th' King.

PIRACQUO
I dare not do so much injustice to

The Prince's bounty, to divide and ow
But half the benefit to his Grace; I not
Extenuate your prevalence at Court, but
His Highness did compassionate my exile,
And I am return'd by his commands, my Lord,
I am his creature for it, and shall sooner
Lose what he hath preserv'd, my life and peace here,
Than doubt his honour, or dispute his power
In my behalf.

RODERIGO
Sir, you are not safe yet,
There has past no seal, I take it, for your pardon.
You hang i'th' air, not fixt to th' roof of heaven,
As when you shin'd a star; take heed you prove
No Comet, a prodigious thing snatch'd up
To blaze, and be let fall agen, upon
Their eyes, that so mistook the region
Where you were plac'd.

PIRACQUO
I know, my Lord, your greatness,
And hold it not becoming, to contest
In language wi'ee; but I am confident—

RODERIGO
Of what?

PIRACQUO
And will wager, if your Grace please,
The to 'ther fifty thousand Ducats, Sir,
That I'll not pay you a Marvedie; if I may
On other honourable terms possess
Your favour, I shall meet your just commands,
But if you set such price upon your smile,
After the Prince's honor to secure me,
I know my self, my fortune, and upon
What strength I must depend.

RODERIGO
I shall, my Lord,
Send you to sea agen.

PIRACQUO
I made a shift, and may agen, my Lord,
Amongst the Merchants.

RODERIGO

Pirate—

PIRACQUO
'Tis confest,
I was so, but your Grace may be inform'd
I was not born to th' trade, I had a soul
Above my fortune, and a toy I took
To lose what was beneath my birth and titles,
Or purchase an estate fit to sustain 'em;
The sea was my Exchequer; for I thriv'd,
I thank my watry Destinies, and commanded
Many a tall ship, won with so much horror,
As possibly would have made your Lordship had you
But in a cloud, or airie scaffold stood
Spectator of our fight) sweat out your soul
Like a thin vapour with the fright, and after
Drop your forsaken body on our deck,
To encrease the number of the dead.

RODERIGO
But we
May deal with you at land agen.

PIRACQUO
With reverence to your blood as 'tis the Kings, withall my age,
My wounds upon me, and that innocence,
The Prince's word hath new created in me,
I do not fear—

RODERIGO
Whom?

PIRACQUO
The Devil.

RODERIGO
I shall conjure down the spirit.

PIRACQUO
Hell hath not art to keep it down.

RODERIGO
So brave?

PIRACQUO
So just.

RODERIGO

Thou talking fool, do'st think I have no stings?

PIRACQUO
I know you are a Statesman, Sir, but he
That fears with his own innocence about him,
Deserves not a protection—

[Offers to go.

RODERIGO
Piracquo,
Stay, I now see thou hast a gallant spirit,
Let me embrace thee, and with this confirm
An honourable friendship; I have not
A thought so base to injure thee.

PIRACQUO
I have—
An easy faith my Lord—

RODERIGO
Farewell—
Noble Piracquo, I have tri'd and found thee.

PIRACQUO
I wo 'not trust you for all this; I know
The Devil's excellent at the hug; your Servant.

[Exit.

[Enter **MANUEL** and **CLARA**, at the other door **MARIA**.

MANUEL
The Princess.

MARIA
I doe not like his Courtship there.
Don Manuel—

[**MANUEL** leaves **CLARA**, and goes to **MARIA**.

RODERIGO
So gratious with my Niece? I'll make him curse
Those smiles—

[Exit.

CLARA

All is not well within me, and the Princess
Was never so unwelcome; they confer
With much delight, or else my fears abuse me.
What hath she in the greatness of her birth,
That I should be so passive? Heaven look on
Our hearts, and if my love want a degree
Of noble heat, when they are both compar'd,
Let what I carry be the Funeral pile,
And my own flame consume it. Ha, the Prince!

[Enter **CARLO**.

I shall betray my self too soon I fear.

CARLO
My sweetest Clara!

MARIA
Either there were no Ladies that could love
In that Court, or you could not want a Mistris.

MANUEL
They are not born with incapacity
Of loving, where they find a worth t'invite:
The fault was in my undesert, that could
Attract no Ladies grace to own me there,
So inconsiderable a servant Madam.

MARIA
There is some hope, you wil not be thought here
Unworthy of a nobler Character;
I doe not think but Clara hath a better
Opinion of your merit.

CARLO
You cannot be so cruel; what could in
My absence interpose, to make your heart
Unkind to those desires at my return?

CLARA
My justice, and the care of both our honours,
I have not lost; nor can Time make me forfeit,
(What Nature, and the Laws of Heaven and Earth
Command me to preserve) my duty Sir.
What is above, would taste ambitious.

CARLO
This was not wont.

CLARA
If any of your smiles,
Or favours Sir before, have led my tongue
To unbecoming boldness, you have mercy:
Some things of error are exalted by
Our bold belief, when Princes make themselves
But merry with their servants, who are apt
To antedate their honour, and expound,
In their own flattery, the text of Princes.

CARLO
But is all this in earnest?

[Enter **RODERIGO** and **ANTONIO**.

RODERIGO
Is not that
Don Manuel with the Princess? Observe Sir.

ANTONIO
They are pleasant.

RODERIGO
Dare he presume?

ANTONIO
Vexation!

CLARA
While I have
The memory of what you are, a Prince,
And dare believe what is as true, as talk'd of,
Your Contract made in Portugall to the Princess
Isabella—

CARLO
No Contract Madam; I confesse,
To please my Father, who engag'd me to
The travel, I did seem to court the Princess,
And with some shadows of a promise, might
Advance her expectation; but here
I left my heart, and dare appeal to thine.

ANTONIO
Madam—

MARIA

Your Graces pardon but a minute.

ANTONIO [To **MANUEL**]
Sir—

MARIA
Nay then I shall repent I ask'd your pardon.

ANTONIO
I ha' done, and will attend your Graces pleasure.

MARIA
I am now at your commands.

[Exeunt.

RODERIGO
Clara his Mistris?

CARLO
Possible! was not that Prince Antonio, Uncle?

RODERIGO
Yes Sir, and gone displeased,
He hath been affronted by that Gentleman.

CARLO
He dares not be so rude.

RODERIGO
He dares be insolent, and court your Sister.

CARLO
How? my Sister? be less ambitious, Manuel.

RODERIGO
Your favours have exalted him too much.

CARLO
But I can change my brow.

RODERIGO
It does become you.

[Exeunt **RODERIGO** and **CARLO**.

MANUEL
The Prince did frown upon me, Madam, you

Are wise, as well as fair, can you resolve
The Prince's riddle?

CLARA
Sir, I have no art
To decypher mysteries, but if I erre not,
He nam'd his Sister.

MARIA
Ha!

CLARA
With caution you should be less ambitious.

MARIA
'Tis so, he's jealous of my courtship there,
It can be nothing else, can it, sweet Madam?
I dare make you the judge of all my thoughts,
Unbosom every counsell, and divest
My soul of this thin garment that it wears,
To let your eye examine it; if you find
Within that great diaphanal an atome
Look black, as guilty of the Prince's anger,
Let him doom me to death, or if that be
Not punishment enough, be you more cruel,
And frown upon me too.

CLARA
If I were judge,
Without such narrow, and severe dissection,
Don Manuel, of your heart, I should declare
Boldly your innocence, and rather than
A frown of mine should rob your thought of quiet,
I would deprive mine eyes of what they honour,
By a more cruel absence.

MARIA
But to be
Assured of so much charity I could wish
My self in some degrees a guilty person,
And stand the Prince's anger; but if I
Be cleer'd in your opinion, I dread not
The malice of accusers; yet if you had
Wav'd my integrity, I had an argument
To have convinc'd you, Madam, that Maria,
Though sacred in her person, was to me
No more enflaming than a piece of Alabaster,
Which some great Master's hand had shap'd a Virgin;

For if you dare believe me, you have won
By your virtue here so much dominion,
There is no room to entertain a guest,
Much less a competition. Oh Madam,
I took so strange a charm in at my eyes
When first your presence made 'em happy, that
To say I only lov'd you, were prophane,
And would detract from that religious honour,
My heart in that first minute promis'd you.

CLARA
I know not in what language, Sir, to dress
My answer, but in that small skill I have,
Sir, of my self, I am not guilty of
Unkind rewards, where I can understand
A fair respect invite 'em; yet if you
But flatter, for it is hard to say, when men
Dissemble not at Court—

MARIA
The curse of Virgins, and
What else can make a Lover miserable
Feed on my heart, that minute I betray
Your faith by any treason of my tongue:
I must not live with your suspicion on me;
Why doe you obscure your face?

CLARA
I doe but hide
Sir an unruly blush that's stoln into
My cheek; I fear a Spy, that hath discovered,
And would tell what complexion my heart has.
Pray leave me.

MARIA
That command
Receiv'd but faint commission from your heart,
From whence those am'rous spies your blushes came;
It had a sound like Virgins, when they teach
A way to be denied. Pardon sweet Madam,
If I presume to interpret my own happiness;
Your eyes are not so kind to obscure themselves
Behind that cloud, they may behold me kiss

[He kisses her hand.

Your hands with this devotion, and not
Repent to be a witness. Did you not

Feel a chast trembling on my lip? with such
A fear doe Pilgrims salute holy Shrines,
And touch the flesh of Martyrs: but this circumstance
Is but the pomp, no essence of affection.
Say, can you love me, Madam? if your tongue
Not us'd to such a dialect, refuse
Articulate consent, a smile will make
No noise, speak that way; I will keep this hand
Both a white pledge, and prisoner, till your eye
Or welcome accent doe redeem it from me;
Or if you still be silent, I'll secure
My fate, and teach your hand without a voice
To chant a Song to Hymen.

[Sings.
What help of tongue need they require,
Or use of other art,
Whose hands thus speak their chast desire,
And grasp each others heart?
Weak is that chain that's made of air,
Our tongues but chafe our breath,
When Palms thus meet, there's no despair
To make a double wreath.
Give but a sigh, a speaking look,
I care not for more noise,
Or let me kiss your hand, the Book,
And I have made my choyce.
Weeping? I'le kiss those drops away.

CLARA
Away—!

MARIA
That eccho was not sweet, yet being thine—

CLARA
I am too much thine.

MARIA
There's no place for fears;
Love is the purest, when 'tis washt in tears.

[Exeunt.

ACT II

SCENE I

An Apartment in the Palace.

Enter **KING** and **RODERIGO**.

KING
Dares he be so insolent allready? we
Shall humble him.

RODERIGO
He durst affront me Sir;
And when I urg'd the folly of his pride,
Tell me, he knew himself, and on what strength
He must depend; words of a dangerous consequence.

KING
My Son hath been too forward.

RODERIGO
He affects him strangely.

KING
Whose undertaking must not bind beyond
The rule of our own greatness.

RODERIGO
Your Son is full
Of honourable thoughts, but being young,
May meet with subtle natures, whose oblique
And partial ends want no dissembled forms
Of duty to betray him. This Piracquo
In his experience of the world, hath art,
And can from every accident extract
A cunning use of time, and dispositions;
And 'tis not to be doubted but the man
Practiz'd in storms, and rapine (by which he
Hath drawn a wealth above your treasury)
May find a minute apt for his revenge
Upon your justice—
He that is a Pirate
In the first act of spoyl he makes, doth open
His conscience at sea, and throws the key
Into the waves.

KING
He hath acquir'd a mighty wealth.

RODERIGO

But who can number their undoings and wet eys
That have been rob'd? how many lives and fortunes
Of your own subjects have increas'd the pile
Of his estate and cruelty? think o' that:
And if you can bring nearer thoughts, and look
Upon your self, your present sums are lean,
Compar'd to what did swell your treasury;
Your customs are less numerous for his thefts,
And your great debts and charge upon your crown,
Are call'd upon, but drouzy with their weight,
They make no answer to the kingdoms clamour.
Some King, to whom the waves had sent a wrack
So great upon his shore, would both secure,
And call the timely benefit, a providence.

KING

'Tis not too late.

RODERIGO

Wise Princes that have law & strength about 'em,
Must take all forfeits; he that is too tame
In Sovergnity, makes treason his own judge,
And gives a patent to be disobey'd.

KING

Let him be sent for streight.

RODERIGO

To hear him plead?
What Traytor did want reasons of defence?
Command him safe first, see his wealth seal'd up
Against the confiscation; Kings must act,
And not dispute their maxims; I could much
Amaze you, Sir, with other argument
To prove Piracquo's insolence; his son
(And 'tis to be believ'd, in things of consequence
Their counsels often meet) Don Manuel,
Hath been ambitious to court Maria,
Your daughter, Sir.

KING

Unsufferable impudence!

RODERIGO

Antonio too suspects him, and what honor
You can maintain with the Prince, & what danger
It may produce; if this resented, and

Proclam'd, beget a War upon your country—
For Treaties are the immunities of Kings,
Subjects adulterate the Prince's coyn,
Not without high injustice, but he that
Doth play the wanton with his royal promise,
Defaceth his own stamp, and teacheth, by
His violation, others not to trust him.

[Enter **ANTONIO** and **MANUEL** fighting. Enter several **LORDS**.

KING
Treason!

MANUEL
Be fearless, Sir, I am provok'd
Beyond the sufferings of a Gentleman.

RODERIGO
Where is the guard? no mischief the result
Of such a skirmish?

MARIA
I was not made for servitude, nor must I
Have patience, when the greatest man is in Spain,
Whose title cannot challenge my subjection,
Throws infamy upon me.

ANTONIO
Do the Kings
Of Spain allow this saucy privilege
Against a Prince.

KING
Not we: To prison with him.

[**MANUEL** is guarded off.

You shall be judge your self, and set the punishment
Upon his insolent act; away with him.

MANUEL
Not hear me? this is tyranny.

RODERIGO
Away, d'ee make a cypher of the King?
Manuel guarded off.

KING

May we
Entreat to know the circumstance?

ANTONIO
I must
Acknowledge, Sir, I had suspicion
Of some attempts by him against my honor,
Which made me first provoke him.

KING
Dare he hope
To keep a thought unpunished?

[Enter **PIRACQUO**.

PIRACQUO
Sir, I met
My Son by your command lead prisoner hence,
It will not unbecome your royall justice,
To let me know his crime, I am no father
To any sin he dares commit against
Your Laws, or person.

KING
You came in good time.
Another guard for him!

[Exit **RODERIGO**.

PIRACQUO
A guard? for what?

KING
You shall know that hereafter.

ANTONIO
I shall beseech, my cause against Don Manuel
May not involve his innocence; my Lord
Piracquo is full of honor.

1ST LORD
The Duke's gone.

2ND LORD
Nay he is right, at the wrong end of a cause still.

ANTONIO
If they be crimes against your state, I am not

To prescribe your Justice, Sir.

KING
Away with him.

[Exit **GUARD** with **PIRACQUO** guarded.

[Enter a **GENTLEMAN** with a letter to **ANTONIO**.

ANTONIO
To me? I have seen this character.

[Exit **ATTENDANT**.

CARLO [within]
Return him at my peril, Sir.

2ND LORD
What do you think of my Lord Piracquo?

[Enter **CARLO** with **PIRACQUO** guarded.

1ST LORD
I think he's gone to prison; yet I think
He's here agen, if that be he; for we are
Not sure of any thing at Court. Now, my Lord—

PIRACQUO
Do any of you know, my Lords, wherefore
I am under guard?

1ST LORD
Not we.

PIRACQUO
I could not satisfie the Prince's question.

2ND LORD
Your sons offence was an affront to th' Prince
Antonio.

PIRACQUO
That was not well; 'twas
Some high provocation made him lose his temper.

1ST LORD
They were at it with their swords.

PIRACQUO

No hurt, I hope?

2ND LORD

The Prince's feather discompos'd, or so.

PIRACQUO

This was not my fault, Gentlemen.

CARLO

Proclame to th' world I'm not your son, take off
Mine and your peoples expectation,
And then 'tis no dishonor; for to be
Believed the Prince at the same time, and one
That dares betray a Gentleman from's Sanctuary,
To be a sacrifice at home, are things
Of inconsistent nature, and destructive.
Charge him with new committed crimes, since I
Gave him my word and honour to secure him,
And there he stands, without an Altar to
Protect him; but far be it from the King,
To make it a new treason to be rich;
It will be thought your avarice to his wealth,
And read in story to your shame for ever,
Piracquo died to pay your debts.

1ST LORD

The Prince
Solicites hard; the King inclines.

CARLO

I know
This doth not, Sir, proceed from your own soul,
But some malignant nature, that hath drop'd,
And would infect your ear with wicked counsell;
'Twas some malicious enemy to me,
And to your fame (as well as Don Piracquo
His life and fortune) hath conspir'd to make
Me less than Prince, and you unfit to be
A King, when once men catch at your inconstancie.
For I must pray you to remember, Sir,
I had your royall promise to confirm
My undertaking for his facts at sea,
And give me leave to say, Sir, this dishonorable
Retreat will stagger all your peoples faith:
A King to break his sacred word, will teach
The great men to be safe without your service;
Who will beleeve your smiles are snares to catch

Their fortunes; and when once the crowd takes sent
Of this, you leave your self no oath to swear by.

2ND LORD
The Prince bestirs himself bravely in your cause.

PIRACQUO
I may do something to reward it, one day.
Sir, shall I speak? not in my own defence;
For since I came to Spain, I have not been
Guilty in thought of any breach of duty;
Nor for my son, if youth or ignorance
Have made him erre, my humble knees beseech
My cause may take no royall beam from him,
That now is pleas'd to be my Advocate,
Your son; in whom there's such an active heat
Of honor, better all my blood was scatter'd
Than you should frown upon him. But I know
If I had payd the Duke your brother, Sir,
But fifteen thousand Ducats—

KING
Ha! what then?

PIRACQUO
I had bought my peace, and been commended by
His Grace to your full pardon.

1ST LORD
Boldly urg'd.

CARLO
Was it his act?

KING
We restore thee,
Piracquo, to thy self, and us; and let
Our largest pardon for all past offences
Be ready for our signature; my brother,
I'll promise reconcil'd too: Carlo, thou
Hast but confirm'd our hope, nor did we purpose
This other than a tryal of thy temper,
Thy gratitude, and jealousie of thy honor:
Preserve them still thus, Carlo, nothing wants
To fix our Kingdoms joy, but the compleating
Thy marriage with the Princess Isabella,
Which shall be done by Proxy, when Antonio
Hath made his courtship perfect with thy Sister.

Who saw the Duke Mendoza? send for him;
He doth too much absent himself.

[Exeunt all but **CARLO**.

CARLO
By Proxy?
The Duke Mendoza's counsell is too busie
To advance that, and Clara is grown cold,
Or seems so, in her cunning to provoke
My flame; but I must teach her how to meet it.
My father may be wrought to a consent
When things are done; forgive me, Isabella,
My first thoughts cannot on thy beauty wait,
I am not master of my love, or fate.

[Exit.

SCENE II

A Room in Mendoza's House.

[Enter **PEDRO**.

PEDRO
Things are not now so desperate, whilst my Lord
Piracquo keeps possession; but if I were
Worthy to advise his Lordship, he should not lose
Much time to settle things, secrets do burn—

[Enter **MENDOZA**.

His grace; now for a fit of jealousie—
I'll be here—

[Walks aside and listens.

MENDOZA
He's troublesome in my eye, and yet I cannot
Endure him from my sight.

PEDRO
That's I.

MENDOZA
Methinks he hath every day a more discovering look,

There's Scaffolds in his face; I shall prevent him,
And send him far enough, with the next Fleet
He goes, the Sea may roar, and crack the Cabbins,
Or he may meet the Calenture; I have heard
Of Hericanoes that have torn up Mountains,
One boysterous enough would strike his Ship
Clean through, a'tother side to the Antipodes,
And that would cure me; all my Art must be
To win him to the Voyage, and not stir
His jealousie; the Knave is apprehensive.

PEDRO
Are you good at that?

[Exit.

MENDOZA
I doe not like his business with Piracquo,
'Tis for no good, I'll break their correspondence;
Piracquo has been honourable, yet
I doe not much confide in him—

[**PEDRO** comes forward.

He's here;
Come hither Pedro.

PEDRO
Your Graces Pleasure?

MENDOZA
What consult
Have you with Don Piracquo?

PEDRO
Please your Grace,
He hath been fishing, some or other have
Infus'd a scruple, I'll engage my life:
But though he be my Kinsman and a Lord
I honour, and from whom I have receiv'd
The promise of a Fortune, and a great one,
Yet, I have said little—

MENDOZA
Hast said any thing?

PEDRO
How could I choose Sir? he did squeez me subtly,

But I was wise, and faithfull to your trust,
He knows no more than I, or you—

MENDOZA
Ha!

PEDRO
Wou'd wish him Sir, let me alone to be cautious.

MENDOZA
Th' art honest Pedro, and I have been studying
How to encourage and reward thy service,
And I have thought of a preferment for thee.

PEDRO
Your Grace was ever bountiful.

MENDOZA
A place
Of honour and command.

PEDRO
That will do well Sir;
And shal I come in as your Churchmen do?
No first-fruits to be paid twice in a year,
No buying of a Jewell at the rate
Of fifteen hundred times the value Sir?

MENDOZA
Remove that care.

PEDRO
That care is well remov'd.

MENDOZA
I have consider'd, that to live at home
My Servant, is to dark thy abilities,
That will abroad shine, and doe services
Worth Spain's acknowledgement.

PEDRO
Abroad? why, must I travell?

MENDOZA
By any means.

PEDRO
Whither, an't please your Grace?

MENDOZA
But to the Indies.

PEDRO
No farther? Columbus did it in 7 years,
And less.

MENDOZA
In the next Fleet thou shalt have an imployment
Shall speak my care of thee, and interest
With his Catholick Majestie; he shall deny
Me hard, but I'll prevail to make thee of
His Council there, and the State Secretary.

PEDRO
This is a mighty honour.

MENDOZA
We may hold
Correspondence still by Letters, thou art wise;
The King shall knight thee too of Calatrava;
How will it joy my heart to write to thee,
Al Signor illustrissimo Don Pedro.

[Enter **GENTLEMAN**.

GENTLEMAN
Sir, the King hath sent for you?

[Exit.

MENDOZA
For me?

PEDRO
Yes, Sir, I could have told your Grace
His Majesty commanded your attendance.

MENDOZA
For what?

PEDRO
I know not that, but I suspect
There hath been some intelligence, however
Go, Sir, it may do worse, and argue guilt,
To be commanded twice.

MENDOZA
Intelligence?
It will be worth my safety to confess.

PEDRO
By no means, Sir, that simplicity
Would rather become me.

MENDOZA
Why? wo't thou confess?

PEDRO
Not, unless you begin; go Sir, an't be
But to prepare his Majesty, for me
To wear the order of the Caletrava;
You have put me, Sir, into the gang of going
This Indian voyage.

MENDOZA
Well, I must to the King.

PEDRO
Shall I attend you?

MENDOZA
Yes—no—do what thou wilt; yet now I think on't
'Twill be as well to go—yet do not neither.

PEDRO
Be chearfull, Sir, why doth your head shake so?

MENDOZA
My head?

PEDRO
It trembles like the Needle of a Sun-dial, d'ee not feel it?

MENDOZA
Ha! yes 'tis here; but do not breath upon me;
I feel the very wind of thy words blow it
To and agen like a Weather-cock; but I must go.

PEDRO.
I will prepare my self for this voyage.
Forget not the Calatrava.

MENDOZA
I would thou wert shipt—

[Exit.

PEDRO
And sunk.
It shall go hard but I'll requite your Lordship.

[Exeunt.

Another Room in the Same.

[Enter **CLARA** and **SERVANT**.

CLARA
A prisoner sayst?

SERVANT.
'Tis a confirm'd report.

CLARA
I fear Prince Carlo's jealousie is cause
Of this; poor Manuel, it will not be
Safe, or seem honorable for me to visit him:
But since I cannot suffer with him, he

[Exit **SERVANT**

Shall hear I dare confine my self to sorrow.

[Enter **SERVANT**.

SERVANT
Madam, the Princess
Maria is coming up the stairs.

CLARA
I must dissemble now my grief, and meet her, yet
I may intreat her Graces mediation
To the King for his enlarge.

[Enter **MARIA**.

MARIA
Let us be private.

[Exit **SERVANT**.

If e'r thou lov'dst me, Clara, now express it.

CLARA
I have an humble sute to your Highness, which
In hope to prosper, will direct my faith,
And services to what you can prescribe me.
Speak your commands.

MARIA
Don Manuel stands committed by the King,
And I would have thy counsel, how I should
Best work his liberty.

CLARA
That, Madam, is
All my petition to your Grace.

MARIA
I know my least desire let fall to th' Prince
Antonio, were enough to engage, and make him
The Orator to effect it, but in honor
I would not contrive him the means, and instrument
To advance his Rival's liberty.

CLARA
Rival, Madam?

MARIA
For I must tell thee, Clara, and with it
Give up the secret of my soul, I love
Don Manuel, I fear, better than my self.

CLARA
You do not mock me, I hope, Madam?

MARIA
No,
By all that Ladies once in love do pray for,
By him thou lov'st, who e'r he be, and this
Kiss (that I rather wish on Manuel's lip,
Would modesty and honor give it privilege
And durst entrust thy faith to carry it to him,
In my experience of thy virtue, Clara)
I speak no fable.

CLARA

It becomes my truth
To answer yours, though not so cheerfully;
I should not much repent, to carry, Madam,
Your kiss to Manuel, but I fear, I should
Forget who sent it. If you have a plot
To raise mirth from my weakness, when you know
How much my heart is his, I yeeld my self
Your triumph, Madam, but the glories of
Your blood, and title are not price enough
To buy him from my thoughts, could you invest
My name with their possession.

MARIA

Doth she love him?
I have destroy'd my own hope then; alas!
Poor Clara, I must pity thee, and for that
Love that hath been between us, I'll apply
To cure thy wound; for mine is not so desperate,
Though I bleed inwards, I confess, since he,
Whom I esteem best, suffers for Maria.

CLARA

Suffer for you? pray Madam, clear this mystery.

MARIA

It is poor Manuel's fortune to affect
Me with a passion great; as mine, and love,
That like a rebell forrageth our soul,
And can obey no law, but what it likes,
Impatient that Antonio lov'd me too,
Made him forget the Prince, and gave the affront,
For which he suffers in the Kings displeasure.

CLARA

No repetition of this story, Madam,
Lest you destroy all my belief in virtue;
It cannot be, you may as soon perswade
That snow, the innocent fleece of heaven, that's born
Upon the fleet wings of some sportive wind,
Is Ethiop's wooll, as call this truth.

MARIA

This will be rudeness, Clara, if you do not
Convince, and with more reason, and with temper.
And 'tis no little wonder, that when I
Have fairly thus disclos'd my thoughts of Manuel,
You should retain a murmuring thought, and dare

Pretend rivality with me.

CLARA
The law
You gave to love, that stoopes to no prerogative
Of birth, or name (mine only a degree
Beneath your own) will answer your disdain,
And justifie my passion; and if reason
And temper (which in vain you think are lost
In me) be assign'd judges, I dare more
Than say I love, I can deserve him—

MARIA
Better?
Fate bring it to a tryall.

CLARA
So just are my affections, I dare make
A Saint my judge.

MARIA
That Judge you make, is not
A friend to so much pride.

CLARA
You are but my accuser, Madam.

MARIA
This affront I must
Remember, Clara, and find time to teach
You know me better.

CLARA
Madam, as you are
The Princess, I can fall thus low, to kiss
Your hand, and pay all duties that become me,
Or your command; but if you think by being
Great, I must own no passion, but in what
Degree you are pleas'd to fix it, nor compare
My soul born with its freedome to affection,
With yours, because one shaft hath wounded both,
I rise my own defender.

MARIA
Thy own ruine
For this presumption.

CLARA

I'll not bribe your mercy,
When you can love as I doe, we may both
Deserve him equally: Oh Manuel!

[Exit **MARIA**.

Though I defend thy honour to the Princess,
Yet he hath scatter'd seeds of jealousie
About my heart, if this ground fertile prove,
I wo'not curse his faith, but my own love.

[Exit.

SCENE IV

A Prison.

MANUEL discovered.

MANUEL
Why should we murmur to be circumscrib'd,
As if it were a new thing to wear fetters?
When the whole World was meant but to confine us;
Wherein who walks from one Clime to another,
Hath but a greater freedome of the Prison;
Our Soul was the first Captive, born to inherit
But her own Chains, nor can it be discharg'd
Till Nature tire with its own weight, and then
We are but more undone to be at liberty.

[Enter **CARLO**.

The Prince, he brings a storm, I see it rising
As Seamen doe, the wind far off.

CARLO
Don Manuel,

MANUEL
You have nam'd a suffering man, but one that holds
His life and death at such an even rate,
No matter which is first employ'd with honour.
I dare submit me to your justice Sir.

CARLO
Your Cause would droop to trust to that, my love

Willing to justifie the choice it made
In thee, hath pleaded better, and prevail'd
With me to bring thee counsel to redeem
Thy self becomingly.

MARIA
Your goodness flows still,
'Twas not the Prince that frown'd.

CARLO
Submit your self to Prince Antonio.

MANUEL
Submit my self?

CARLO
Ask him forgiveness.

MANUEL
I must be guilty first of an offence,
Ere my tongue be so base, and ask a pardon.

CARLO
Then I must chide you Manuel; deny
This trivial satisfaction? your crime
Will upon second thoughts be much enlarg'd,
Nor will the Prince be ever thought to merit
His birth and name, unless he kill thee for't,
'Tis an affront of so supreme a nature.

MANUEL
Hath it no name Sir?

CARLO
Dost not shake to ask it?
Are you Sir a fit Rivall for the Prince?
Abstract that she's my Sister, which consider'd,
Carries so vast a guilt against the Kings,
Mine, and Maria's honour, all thy bloud
Mixt with repentance cannot purge; you are
Instructed Sir.

MANUEL
Not yet, to know my self
Conscious of any action should contract
The Prince's brow, or yours, much less deserve
The horrid name of guilt against the Kings,
Yours, and Maria's honour.

CARLO
Did not you Sir court my Sister?

MANUEL
Never Sir.

CARLO
Doe not you love her?

MANUEL
Heaven in that word includes all that we owe
His precept; 'Tis my justice, Sir, to love her;
But with a greater distance, than she is
From me remov'd by birth; and if her smile
Meant the reward of my attendance, Sir,
At any time have met with false observers,
Their tongues, and no audacious thought of mine,
Or application, are in fault; I have,
Beside the lesson of my birth, been taught
A piety from your favours, Sir, to know
My self their creature, and with humble thoughts
To shew my gratitude, not proudly assume
(Could she descend) a Courtship to Maria,
Who by the King, & every good mans vote,
Is meant a sacred pledge to Portugal,
To chain two kingdoms.

CARLO
If this, Manuel,
Be truth—

MANUEL
Without condition of my liberty,
Or dread of what Antonio shall attempt
In his revenge, my soul dare wth ith an oath
Confirm it at the Altar.

CARLO
This doth please me.
Possess thy first place in my friendship, Manuel;
Antonio shall embrace thee too, his ear
And mine have been abus'd.

MANUEL
There was
A providence upon our Swords, that meant
Less fatall than his passion shew'd, when we

Last met, against whose weapon threatning me first,
The safety of my fame, more than my life,
Call'd up my just defence.

CARLO
I do beleeve thee;
To what a loss of virtue, and of blood
Credulity engageth? this shall be
No more thy dwelling; Prince Antonio
Shall for thy honor make it his own act,
Who yet believes thy interest in Maria
Hath made his Courtship vain, and will I fear,
Not presently admit thy innocence
Into his quiet faith, but I'll convince him.

MANUEL
If he but knew my heart, he should not need
Much argument; no man can love with honour,
And let his thoughts divide upon two Mistrisses.
I have contracted love—

CARLO
With whom? may Time,
When this World fails, and Nature grows decrepit;
Present it to Eternity.

MANUEL
This prayer opens my heart, and all the wealth within it,
Commands me draw the Curtain from her name,
That you may read my Clara,
And I shall beseech your Graces smile—

CARLO
Your Clara? what
The Duke Mendoza's Daughter?

MANUEL
You have nam'd her.

CARLO
No, I am i'th' dark still, speak agen,
Or rather say, thou hast mistook, it is
Some other Clara, and not the Lady
I understand.

MANUEL
Life cannot bribe me with another wealth,
Or death with all his horrours make me desert

That name.

CARLO
What a strange Sea-breach has
This little storm of breath made here allready?
I was taking pains to unconcern the jealousie
Of Antonio, and find him my own Rivall;
Thou hadst been kinder to have lov'd Maria
My Sister, though Antonio had sworn
Thy death, and the Kings anger with my own
Had met thee like a torrent, than presum'd
This interest in Clara.

MANUEL
I see no
Such mighty danger in't.

CARLO
I'll tell thee, Manuel,
Thou hast invaded all my joys, I love her.

MANUEL
Honor forbid it, Sir.

CARLO
Honor's a dream,
And a cold everlasting sleep must chain
My soul up; for if once it wake, and know
What thou hast torn from't, it will vex it self
Into a flame, and turn thee into ashes.

MARIA
Never til now unhappy, with my weight
I see my self now bearing down before me,
A rotten part of some prodigious mountain
Into the sea, with which I shall soon mingle.

CARLO
Collect thy self betimes, and give her back
Unsullied with thy clame, release thy own,
And with her, every thought as much a virgin
As her soul was, when first I courted her,
Or thou art lost—

MANUEL
With greater justice, Sir,
Command to uncreate my self, as call
My faith or heart agen.

CARLO
How?

MANUEL
Sir, my life,
The cement that doth hold this frame together,
You have power to melt, or but command my exile,
And I may live far off, and be forgotten
By all, but Clara; but to ask that back,
Which with the full consent of heaven I gave her
(And in exchange receiv'd her equall vow)
I dare not, or if I had will, to be
So false to honour, 'tis within my heart
So rivetted, I may with as much innocence
Commit a rape, or murder, as attempt it.

CARLO
You have no doubt a valour too, that dare
Love with so fierce a resolution.

MANUEL
When I am master of my sword, I dare
Not draw it against you; but he that lives
Beneath you, may have little time to wish
Himself unmade that would divorce us.

CARLO
Leave me, leave me—

[Exit **MANUEL**

How many loves are shaken with one tempest?
And if one suffer, ruin'd all? I know
The faith he bears me, and the reverence
He gives my blood, will never be provok'd
To fight against my person; but I must not
By tameness give my self a publike wound;
He shall be master of his sword and freedom,
And then let fate determine; Clara must
Be mine, or make a Bridegroom of his dust.

[Exit.

ACT III

An Apartment in the Palace.

Enter **GENTLEMEN** of Prince Antonio, preparing a banquet.

1ST GENTLEMAN
Prince Carlo's not come yet.

2ND GENTLEMAN
My Lord Piracquo
And his son Manuel are expected too.

1ST GENTLEMAN
I wonder at this hasty reconcilement;
We did imagine it as possible
The two Poles should have met, as they together
Friends at a Banquet.

2ND GENTLEMAN
In my opinion, peace, and wine, and musick,
Are more convenient for the naturall body,
Than swords or guns.

1ST GENTLEMAN
And for the politick too,
If men were but so wise to like, and cherish
Their own estates: If I had all the Plate
In the Indies, I'd not give a silver spoon
To have my head cut off.

2ND GENTLEMAN
Why is not the great Duke Roderigo here?

1ST GENTLEMAN
Who, the Kings Evil Genius? he was
Invited, but excus'd himself.

2ND GENTLEAMN
Why, there's
A Statesman, that can side with every faction,
And yet most subtly can untwist himself
When he hath wrought the business up to danger.
He lives within a labyrinth, some think
He deals with the devil, and he looks like one,
With a more Holiday face.

1ST GENTLEMAN

But he hath so behav'd himself,
That no man now dare much confide in him.
They are come.

[Music within.

[Enter **ANTONIO, CARLO, PIRACQUO, MANUEL.**

ANTONIO
Don Manuel, the Prince hath made me know
My error, and your worth.

MANUEL
He has too much honor'd me,
And you have reason to command for this
The service of my life.

ANTONIO
You are not pleasant, Sir—[To **CARLO**]
My Lord Piracquo.

PIRACQUO
Your Highness humble servant.

CARLO
All is not
Reconcil'd here, I but suppress a flame,
To give it vent more dangerous [Aside].

ANTONIO
A free welcome to all;
Sit, and some wine; this Musick is not
Sprightly enough: To his Majesty of Spain—

[Drinks.

PIRACQUO
He that doth pledge the Kings health with a murmur
May his next thirst inflame him to drink poyson.

[Drinks.

CARLO
The King hath a true servant in Piracquo.

MANUEL
He that is not, had never sense of honor;
And may he perish all but soul, that dares

Harbour a thought disloyall. To your Highness—

[Drinks.

ANTONIO
Give me another:
This wine looks cheerful as my heart, to drink
The Princess fair Maria's health.

[Drinks.

CARLO
My turn
Will come, Sir, to be gratefull.

ANTONIO
Here my Lord.

PIRACQUO
May swift time perfect by your sacred Loves,
The happiness of both kingdoms!

[Drinks.

MANUEL
May that day,
That seals your glorious Hymen, Sir, be ever
Holy within our Calendar, and beget
A faith, that all things then begun, may prosper!

[Drinks.

ANTONIO
I thank thee, Manuel.

CARLO
Sir, you may
Believe Don Manuel's language, and his heart
Are twins, they bear one date of time, & sense.
You must now give me leave, Sir, to requite
You in part; A health to the King of Portugal;
Let it move this way, Manuel.

[Drinks.

MANUEL
It shall
With humble thoughts be entertain'd—you honor me.

PIRACQUO
It is but Justice Manuel; for when Spain
Would not acknowledge, nor allow us being,
Our lives were welcome there, till better stars
Sent him, to whose bounty we ow all that's left us.

CARLO
No more o'that my Lord, I am very confident,
In any honorable cause, you dare
Express your faith to me; and for your son,
We two have been companions, I dare say,
Our hearts are toucht by one Magnetick virtue,
And such a sympathy, I cannot wish
What's dearest to me, but he flies t'embrace it.

MANUEL [aside]
I like not this—

CARLO
Manuel, begin a health:
We have had my Sisters and the Kings already,
Name your own Mistris for the next.

MANUEL
I should conclude her worthy of remembrance,
If one were first preferr'd. Will your Grace please Sir,
To let me have the honor—

ANTONIO
Come, to me.

MANUEL
To the white hand of fairest Isabella.

[Drinks.

ANTONIO
Would she were
Present to thank you Manuel.

CARLO
'Tis an affront, as Clara were his own
Allready; ha! civilitie and honor
Prescribe me patience, dares he insult?
When this hath had the ceremony, Manuel,
'T shall be my office to remember Clara;
I must have time to quit the favour, Sir,

Y'ave done my Mistris; in your ear; though I
Was pleased to reconcile you to the Prince,
And order your enlargement, Clara must
Be mine, or one of us be nothing; you
May think on't yet.

MANUEL
I have Sir, and to shew
How much I can obey, and that I have not
Intruded like a thief upon your treasure,
And filcht her heart away, 'tis now within
Her choice agen, if you prevail upon
Her kinder thoughts, I can sit down despis'd.

CARLO
Thou art my best friend now. Antonio—
Me-thinks we are not pleasant—if she should
Be a little obstinate, it would become,
And speak the bravery of thy soul, and service,
To use some language for me, wo't thou Manuel?
Thou dost not know the sufferings of my soul
For Clara.

MANUEL
But I pitty 'em.

CARLO
'Tis new balsam
Into my wounds; where is the health, Piracquo?
I feel new spirits dancing in my blood,
The health begun to Clara languisheth,
Why should I want it, Gentlemen?

ANTONIO
It was nam'd
By Manuel to my Sister Isabella;
Prince Carlo, you forget.

CARLO
To Isabella?
Your Graces pardon, I confess my error,
I forgot her indeed, but could your wishes
Translate that Princess hither, she should be
A witness of my honourable thoughts.

[Music within.

[Enter **ISABELLA** with **LADIES**.

What Magick's this? do any know that face?

PIRACQUO
'Tis very like the Princess Isabella.

CARLO
I would she were a Ghost; Antonio,
Have you got enchantments?

[Rising.

ISABELLA
You may stay, Sir.

CARLO
I love not to converse with spirits.

MARIA
Sir,
This is no shadow.

CARLO
It is to me, Sir.
Meet me at Clara's, or be lost to honour.

[Exit.

ISABELLA
It was your Counsel brother, that reserv'd me
For this first entertainment. My good Lord
Piracquo, and Don Manuel, you seem not
So much affrighted, as the Prince.

PIRACQUO
A devil
In such a shape could never fright me, Madam;
But persons of your quality shift not so
Much air without a noise; the motion
Of Princes has much rumor to attend it.

ISABELLA
I chose to come so private, I arriv'd
The City but last evening.

MARIA
You have much
Honour'd Madrid.

ISABELLA
Why, how now brother, are
You frighted too?

ANTONIO
Yes, and do sweat at soul,
To see our selves neglected.

ISABELLA
Some are not fortified against a sudden accident;
In my desert, and innocence, I can
Interpret nothing yet in my dishonour,
Since joyes have extasies sometimes, and with
Their rapture may transport our senses from us,
As soon as any other passion.
Besides, I heard him wish me here a witness
Of honourable thoughts, he has but now
Remov'd his person, to acquaint the King,
With greater preparation to receive
A Guest so unexpected.

PIRACQUO
But I like not the Prince's humor, you
Had whisperings Manuel I observ'd.

MANUEL
I shall
Keep nothing Sir in Clouds from you.

ANTONIO
Thou sha't direct me Isabella, wee'l to Court
My Lord Piracquo, Manuel.

ISABELLA
How ere
I put a valiant brow on his neglect,
And seem to make a gloss in his defence,
My soul is sick with fear [aside].

ANTONIO
Come Isabella.

PIRACQUO
We both attend your grace.

[Exit.

SCENE II

An Apartment in the Palace.

[Enter **RODERIGO**.

RODERIGO
My engines want success, Piracquo is
Restor'd to his full being, and his Son
At large, and reconcil'd by Carlo's act.
My Nephew had been better to have wak'd
A sleeping Dragon, than have cross'd my aims;
He has rescu'd them, but drawn upon his bosome
As many wounds as policy and my
Revenge can make. I was too tame, to strike
At useless Shrubs, that hinder not my prospect;
My thoughts should have no study but a Kingdome;
It is my Heaven, and this young Cedar spread
Betwixt my eyes, and it; I have already
Betray'd his love to Clara, and the King
That hath made up an Idol to himself
Of honour, is inflam'd to my own wishes;
I know the Prince will be impatient
To hear his Mistris tost by the Kings anger,
And he may leap into some disobedience,
That may be worth my second charge to sink him;
And then Piracquo, Manuel, and the Kingdome
Shall stoop to my devotion; yet I carry
A smiling brow to all, and please the King,
To think I am reconcil'd.

[Enter **CARLO**.

My Nephew—

CARLO
Where is the King?

RODERIGO
Where I left him displeas'd, and was now coming
To Prince Antonio's Lodgings to acquaint you.

CARLO
With what?

RODERIGO

Have you contracted love with Duke Mendoza's
Daughter, the Lady Clara?

CARLO
What officious
Tongue hath been bold to mention her?

RODERIGO
He has
Had some intelligence, and is almost grown
Wild with the strange resentment, I not knowing
What to object against his passion, thus
Surpriz'd, you may believe apply'd what lenitives
My understanding could collect o'th' sudden,
With confidence, when you came to give account,
The accusation would fall off, and he
Appear too credulous against your honour.

CARLO
It were no treason to Castile, my Lord,
If I confest this mighty fact.

RODERIGO
'Tis justice
If you doe love her honourably, to avow it.

CARLO
Isabella is no Angel.

RODERIGO
Nor is Clara
Of an extraction to digrace a Prince.

CARLO
Though he be my Father, he did not
Beget my Soul; who's with him?

RODERIGO
I left the Duke Mendoza.

CARLO
Has he made
Complaint o'me? 'tis well; let me preserve
Good Uncle still your loving thoughts; it is
In vain to move my Father now.

RODERIGO
There is

I way, if you could but dissemble, Sir,
To set your wishes right, and Letters may
Be so contriv'd to Portugall.

CARLO
The Princess
Is here allready Uncle.

RODERIGO
Isabella?

CARLO
Now with Antonio, and I am lost.

RODERIGO [aside]
Would thou wert never to be found agen.

CARLO
I must doe something.

RODERIGO
The Princess thus
Affronted may be worth my own ambition.
Calm thoughts attend you Sir.

[Exit.

[Enter **MENDOZZA**.

MENDOZA
I'm glad I came so well off from the King,
His anger made me tremble, I was jealous
Of more discovery, when he nam'd the Prince:
This Treason is a kind of a quotidian,
It leaves a man no intervall; I durst
Not mention Pedro at all, for fear
The King had skill in Cabala; I'm afraid
There's something in the very name, that may
With a small key be open'd to my danger.

CARLO
You are well met my Lord, doe you know me?

MENDOZA [coming forward]
Know you Sir? yes I know you for—

CARLO
For what?

MENDOZA
The Prince, I hope; now I'm betray'd for certain,
Yet if he know it, he will not be so furious.

CARLO
Are you so much an enemy to your self,
To tell the King?

MENDOZA
I tell the King? alas
I dare not tell it to my Ghostly Father,
I have more regard to you, and my own life,
My Family's undone by it.

CARLO
By what Sir?

MENDOZA
Nay if you know not, I know not neither, Sir;
What doe you mean?

CARLO
Am not I worthy in your opinion
Your Daughter Clara's love?

MENDOZA [aside]
Oh, is that all?

CARLO
But you must dote, and tell the King on't.

MENDOZA
I? I disclaim it, by my life and honour.

CARLO
I thought you had lov'd me Sir.

MENDOZA
He is a Traitour
That dares accuse me; now I may speak boldly;
My Blood and Fortune have a little name
I'th' World, to which make an addition of
My Life, my Daughter Clara too, were these
In balance against you, they would be light,
And their whole loss repaird, to see you happy:
If this be false, a Whirlwind snatch me Sir,
And let me hang in some prodigious Cloud

'Twixt Earth and Heaven.

CARLO
This is a bold expression.

MENDOZA
But I must tell you Sir, for your own sake,
I would not have you love my Daughter Clara,
Were she in beauty, person, and all ornaments,
Fortune and Nature could bestow, more excellent
Than Isabella.

CARLO
Why an't please your Wisedome?

MENDOZA
Sir in my love to you, and Isabella,
My duty to your Father, and the Kingdome,
Nay for my Daughter's sake, and all my hope
Of after-joyes, and for one other reason
Above all these, which I conceal; yet I
Complain'd not to the King.

CARLO
Excluding me,
Your Grace can be content, Don Manuel
Should have your Daughter.

MENDOZA
Rather than your Highness,
I know a reason for't.

CARLO
I must so too.

MENDOZA
Your Grace shall pardon me at this time.

CARLO
I wo'not Sir.

MENDOZA
If you'l needs have it, I have made a vow
I wo'not ask my Daughter blessing Sir;
If you two meet, and marry, she may live
To be a Queen, and then I'll kneel to her,
Which is not in the Oath of my Allegiance.

CARLO
The old man raves.

[Exit.

[Enter **KING, MARIA.**

MENDOZA
The King.

CARLO
He shall not see me
Till I know all my fate.

[Exit.

KING
How doe you like the Prince Antonio?

MARIA
Sir, if you allow me freedome—

KING
You enjoy it.

MARIA
His Person, Bloud, and expectations, are
High as the wishes of a Queen, and I
With pious gratitude acknowledge all
My duty, and my prayers a just return
To your great care; but give me Sir your pardon,
If I prefer some thoughts that prompt me to
A better choyce.

KING
A better choyce? look back
Upon that character your breath but now
Deliver'd in his honour.

MARIA
I confirm it;
But when you hear me humbly beg I may
Perform religious duties Sir to Heaven,
You wil think nature hath a place beneath 'em:
If I could find any consent to marriage,
Antonio would prefer himself the first
To my election: but if you were pleas'd—

KING
You would be a Nunn?

MARIA
That hath exprest my wishes.

KING
So I should
Affront the Prince: how long Maria has
This fit of your Religion held you? ha!
No more, least I suspect this a pretence
To hide your love plac'd otherwise unfitly,
If I find where your heart is wandring—

MARIA
It knows obedience better, and your name,
Than to choose any path leads not to honour.

KING
I must direct it then to love Antonio.
My Children are turn'd rebell.

MARIA
Sir I hope
My offer with your leave, to dedicate
My life to prayer, and Virgin-thoughts, will merit
A better name.

KING
Your brother Carlo too
Will find himself at loss, if he collect not
Himself, and make our Royall Promise good
To Isabella; while my studies are
To make the Kingdome firm by our alliance
With Portugall, be courts the Lady Clara.

MARIA [aside]
I would she were his Bride, so I had Manuel.

KING
And you at the same time, and height of both
The Kingdoms expectations, would take a Cloister,
Is this to pay obedience to a Father,
Whose cares have kept him wake to make you happy?

MARIA
Goodness forbid, that Carlo or Maria
Should move me to just anger.

KING
This is virtue.

[Enter a **LORD** and whispers to the **KING.**

MARIA
He is passionate, and Love that makes all Ladies
Apt and ingenious to contrive, cannot
Inspire or help me with an heart to advance
A little hope.

KING
It cannot be! Maria,
We are surpriz'd, the Princess Isabella
Is privately arriv'd, and come to Court:
Where is our Son? all should prepare to meet her.

[Exeunt.

SCENE III

A Room in Mendoza's House.

[Enter **CARLO** and **CLARA**.

CARLO
You may believe I trifle not.

CLARA
The Princess Isabella come?

CARLO
Now if but Clara think I honour her,
And instantly accept what I am willing
In presence of the Priest and Heaven to give her,
The Ceremony waits to make all perfect.

[Enter **MANUEL**.

CLARA
I dare not Sir.

CARLO
Say but you love, and that will teach you valour;
I bring not only proof of my own loyalty,

Which if examin'd must invite thy faith,
But thy security, a Release from Manuel;
His soul is on my side, and comes to render
In pity of thy wound, a balm into
Thy breath; be gentle Clara.

CLARA
A Release? of what?

MARIA
Of all, thy Promise hath made mine;
Observe me wisely Clara, and distinguish,
As far as honour will permit, how long,
And with what bleeding thoughts the Prince affects thee;
For I have look'd into his soul, and back
Upon the feeble merits of my self,
And therefore giving thy own Vows agen,
I dis-engage their strength to bind thee Clara,
And to that sweetness thy first bosome had,
Remit thy quiet thoughts.

CARLO
Th'art just.

CLARA
Pray give
Me leave to understand this mystery,
To give me back all those assurances
Of Love my Promise made, I'll not dispute
For what unworthiness I am neglected.

MARIA
I dare not be so impious.

CLARA
Then here I take
My liberty again.

MARIA
You have it.

CLARA
Now I with safety of my honor, may
Choose where I please.

MARIA
You may.

CLARA
And you desire it;
You have power I must confess to give me from you
Into my own possession, but no title
Now to direct my heart, then though I meet
My own despair, here I give Clara back,
And with new Vows as strong as my Religion,
And Love can make, contract my self agen
To Death, or Manuel.

CARLO
A Conspiracy!

CLARA
I have resign'd no interest in him,
And by new choyce—am not my own agen.

CARLO
So, so, it is as possible in our destinies
We should enjoy her both, as live together,
When Clara is thy Bride.

CLARA
That sound was tragical;
Oh call those fatal words agen, and think
That if with safety of my faith I cannot
Meet your desires already, you will force
My soul to greater distance, by destroying
What most I love; I know you doe but fright me.

MARIA
If I be mark'd for your revenge, I dare not
Think you will stain your honour, to contrive
My death ignobly.

[They whisper]

CLARA
What was that he mention'd?
Sir, by your name and blood I charge you hear me,
By these (your rage compels) a Virgins tears,
I can kneel too, take your revenge on me,
'Tis I that have offended, for your sake
He did return the interest I gave him,
But 'twas not in his power to revoke
Himself made mine, nor dare I quit possession.

CARLO

I have but tryed thy virtue, Manuel
And I are friends.

CLARA
That was a heavenly language.

CARLO
Our swords shall serve to nobler uses, Clara,
I'll not disturb the progress of your Mariage;
And since I see you're fixt so gloriously,
Proceed to your own Hymen, I'll attend you,
And witness all your holy rites.

CLARA
Blest change!
What prayers and duty can reward his goodness?

CARLO
I hope you'll not deny for my past service,
Madam, your smile upon me, which shall be
A triumph after all my wounds receiv'd,
And boast a glory next to be your husband;
For I consider now I am unfit.
Farewell, we may salute. Remember, Manuel,
The time and place.

[Exit.

CLARA
What was it the Prince whisper'd?

MARIA
Nothing, Madam,
To fright your cheek to paleness.

CLARA
I do tremble.

MARIA
Were all this reconcilement a disguise,
And that he meant revenge, should time and place
Fit his inteuts, and I should meet his anger,
·t this secure thy peace, his honor will
Not let him wound me basely, and when I
Lift up a sword 'gainst him, fate let me die.

[Exeunt.

A Room in Mendoza's House.

PEDRO seated at a table.

PEDRO
My Lord is coming to my chamber, he
Has been with the King, I see my self allready
Knight of the order of the Calatrava,
And my Commission sign'd for the State Secretary.
I am not the first servant of the Court
Has kept his Lord in aw; these Secrets are
An excellent curb to ride a Statesman with,
That is not come to the art of poysoning.
I know he wishes heartily I were hang'd;
I tried him once for the wars; to find his pulse,
And I was listed Captain, before some
The General knew had been seven years in service
(As Ushers to right honourable Ladies)
There was his Graces commendations
To a Field-officer, that should drill me out,
The first to dye, with honor on some onslaught;
So quitted that preferment.

[Enter **MENDOZA**.

He is come; I'll take no notice.

MENDOZA
If he liv'd at the t'other end of th' world,
He might betray me in the next packet: Ha!

PEDRO
Item I bequeath—

MENDOZA
What art thou doing?

PEDRO
Only making up my Will, Sir; and my self
Ready for the Indies; 'tis a long voyage,
And therefore I would settle every thing
Before I go; if your Grace please to honor me,

I would make you my Executor.

[Rises and comes forward.

MENDOZA
But when,
Will you dye Pedro? Ha!

PEDRO
Sir, there be storms,
Abroad, and who does know how soon the waves
May rore, and crack the cabins?

MENDOZA
Ha!

PEDRO
There may be Calentures, my Lord, and twenty
Devices to be met at sea, beside
The land diseases; there be Hericanoes
Are boisterous enough to tear up mountains,
And strike a ship clean through o' t' other side
To the Antipodes.

MENDOZA
He deals with the devil, and knows my thoughts.
There's no hast to make your will, I have
Consider'd o' the business, and truth is,
I cannot find my heart willing to part with thee,
So far thou hast been faithful; we will live
And die together.

PEDRO
By no means, my Lord:
I am resolv'd I will not live in Spain
A moneth, for as much plate as the next Fleet
Brings home; no, I beseech your Grace excuse me.

MENDOZA
Why Pedro?

PEDRO
If your Grace please I shall be Knighted,
Or have the Office you have promis'd, do't,
And do't betime, it will be worse for both else.

MENDOZA
You do not threaten to reveal the business?

PEDRO
'Lass, there be other matters, Sir, as dangerous
And if you love your self, or honor, finish—
I cannot help it.

MENDOZA
I am all a bath!
Pedro, why dost thou fright me so? if thou
Be'st honest, ther's no mortal ean betray us.

PEDRO
Worse, worse than that; let me go travel, Sir,
And far enough; it is not possible
That I should stay, and you preserve your wits.

MENDOZA
The reason?

PEDRO
It will make you mad to hear it, Sir,
But 'tis my desperate fate, the stars command it;
Would I had never seen—

MENDOZA
What?

PEDRO
A face that I could name.

MENDOZA
If it concerns not
The other mystery, let me hear it, Pedro,
I will be arm'd.

PEDRO
Why then you'll cut my throat;
You cannot hold your hand; pray let me go,
And you may save all yet.

MENDOZA
Thou dost torment me.

PEDRO
And yet it is no fault of mine, directly,
We are all flesh and blood—oh Sir.

MENDOZA

Out with it.

PEDRO
You'll curse me when you know it.
I would your Grace would guess, but 'tis impossible;
'Tis working to get out, I am—

MENDOZA
Well sayd.

PEDRO
Oh Sir, I am—I am—in love! Now 'tis out.

MENDOZA
That all?

PEDRO
All? a Pistol to a Maravidi you draw
Your Rapier presently upon me, and
If I name but the party, will not have
The patience to foin, but tilt it at me.
Sir, do not know't; what will become of me?
It will be safer, Sir, to hoist sails yet,
No matter whither, So I never come
Agen; for if I see one face too often,
Both you, and I, and she's undone: I have
Beaten my self already, fasted, prayed,
Been drunk, and pray'd agen, nothing will kill
Concupiscence—oh Sir.

MENDOZA
Why, this is raving.

PEDRO
I, you may call it what you please, but here
She lies a cross that must, or doe the deed,
Or make poor Pedro miserable.

MENDOZA
How he sweats?
Pedro do not despair, this feaver may
Be cur'd, it may.

PEDRO
Indeed you can do much;
For to say truth, your Grace is both acquainted,
And has no small command upon the party.

MENDOZA
Nay then be confident—who is't?

PEDRO
It is—shall I name her?

MENDOZA
By my honor I will beat thee else.

PEDRO
Why so then;
The pretty soul, I will confess to you,
Whom, if I stay, I must—

MENDOZA
Enjoy; this such a business?

PEDRO
Is—is—Clara, your Graces one, & only daughter.

MENDOZA
Ha!

[Draws.

PEDRO
I told you this afore, but do not do't, Sir, now,
I rather look for't in the next sallad,
Or in my mornings draught; there's spice i' your closet;
Or we have Spanish figs.

MENDOZA
Thou most unheard-of impudence! how can'st hope
I should not cut thy head off? sirrah, rascal.

PEDRO
To these things humane nature has been prone;
But if you kill me, Sir, there is a schedule,
A Secret in a bag of writings, left
In a friends hand—nay I did look for this,
There is an Inventory of Goods were stoln;
The Anno Domini, with Aetatis suae
Set down, the day o'th' moneth, and place remembred,
If these do not revenge my death—

MENDOZA
Why so; a pox upon thee—yet come hither,
And let me cut thy tongue out.

PEDRO
I confess
I am not fit to marry, Sir, a Lady of
Her Princely birth and fortune, all consider'd;
Alas, I know I am a wreth—but—

MENDOZA
Thou wouldst have her to be thy whore, & me
Thy pander to speak for thee—rogue, devill,
I must kill thee, there is no remedy.

PEDRO
Hold, you mistake me, Sir, 'tis no such business.

MENDOZA
What wouldst thou have then?

PEDRO
I would go beyond sea, I, to the Indies, Sir,
Or turn a Haddack by the way; send me
To the new Islands, or Japan.

MENDOZA
From whence you may send Letters to the King;
No sirrah, I'll not trust you.

PEDRO
'Tis a hard case, my Lord, I have dangerous sailing
Betwixt your Graces Scylla and her Caribdis.

MENDOZA
I dare not kill him; why do I not kill my self then?
No, I wo'not, I will talk reason to him;
Come hither sirra, my tormentor.

PEDRO
I Sir—

MENDOZA
If your hot blood must have a cooler, will
None serve your rogues turn, but my daughter Clara?
Say thou art mad—

PEDRO
I have too many senses.

MENDOZA

Or if your wantonness must be confin'd
Within my walls—

PEDRO

The more my sorrow—but I'll try my Lord,
If you will give me leave, for your sake, Sir,
Among her Gentlewomen, what I can do
To conjure down my devil, I will take
Some physick too, Sir, every thing will help;
Would I were whipt, my Lord—

MENDOZA

Whipt with a vengeance?

PEDRO

But I am griev'd
For your vexation, and my scurvy fortune;
But if there be a wench, a witch, a medicine
Above ground, that can give me any charm,
Your Grace shall hear no more on't—So, your pardon.
And now my Lord, let your unworthy servant
Have leave to ask one question; does not your Grace
Suspect me monstrously? nay d'ee not think
I do presume too much upon your fears?
And that the knowledge of this Secret makes
Me bold and saucy, my good Lord?

MENDOZA

'Tis all too true, but 'tis not in my brain
To help't, unless I take some course to kill thee.

PEDRO

How?

MENDOZA

I fear I shall be driven to't; one fit
Like this will work my impatience up: look to't.

PEDRO

Why, then I'll tell your Grace an easy way
To remove all your jealousie, and never
Trouble your brain with study how to kill me,
A most compendious way.

MENDOZA

I would I knew it.

PEDRO

'Tis but my going to the Court, my Lord,
And if you be not cur'd within an hour
After I have told the King a story, how
Your wife the Duchess lost—I ha' done—
Fear nothing.

[**MENDOZA** appears alarmed.

[Enter **LORD**.

LORD
Is not Prince Carlo here?

MENDOZA
Not here, my Lord.

LORD
'Tis the Kings pleasure you attend him presently,
Your daughters presence is expected too
Among the Ladies, for the entertainment
Of Princess Isabella, new arriv'd the Court.

MENDOZA
We humbly wait to kiss his hand.

PEDRO
Shall I attend?

MENDOZA
I am resolv'd now not to sleep without thee,
And in the day, I'll look upon thee, Pedro,
As thou wert my great Seal, and I thy keeper.

PEDRO
Yet I may give you a slip.

MENDOZA
We'll to Clara:
The Princess Isabella come so private, ha! Pedro?

PEDRO
I am here, my Lord.

[Exeunt

SCENE II

A Solitary Spot without the City.

[Enter **MANUEL.**

MARIA
This is the place by his commands to meet in;
it has a sad and fatal invitation.
A Hermit that forsakes the world for prayer,
And solitude, would be timorous to live here.
There's not a spray for birds to perch upon;
For every tree that over-looks the vale,
Carries the mark of lightning, and is blasted.
The day which smil'd as I came forth, and spread
Fair beams about, has taken a deep melancholy,
That fits more ominous in her face than night;
All darkness is less horrid than half light.
Never was such a scene for death presented,
And there's a ragged mountain peeping over
With many heads, seeming to crowd themselves
Spectators of some Tragedy; but I'll
Prevent 'em all; though my obedience
Instructed me to wait here, it shall not
Be brib'd to draw my sword against the Prince;
And in his honor I am safe, how e'r
This sense of Clara's loss transport him, 'tis not
Within his nature to be impious.
And if I gain his friendship, I return
With triumph to my Clara.
Within—help, help.

[Enter **CELIO**, Prince Carlo's Page.

CELIO
Oh help, Don Manuel, help for heavens sake.

MARIA
Celio the Princes page? where is the Prince?

CELIO
Oh Sir, I fear he's slain.

MARIA
By whom?

CELIO
The Devil, or one not very much unlike him,
A More, that basely set upon him, sure

He has dispatcht the Prince, he persues me,
And if he have, Death shall be welcome to me,
For I am not fit to live, and lose my Master.
He's here, and his sword bloudy.

[Enter **CARLO** like a Moor.

MARIA
Villain! were all thy bloud rivers of balm,
Or such a floud as would restore a life
To the departed World, it should be all
A sacrifice to Carlo.

[They fight. **CARLO** falls.

CELIO
Hold, hold Don Manuel.

MARIA
Canst thou be merciful to the Princes Murderer

CELIO
Curse on my Duty to obey so far.
My Lord, the Prince is slain, you are wounded too.

MARIA
The Prince!

CARLO
Don Manuel, I forgive thee.

MARIA
Pray Heaven this be a Dream; for if my hand
Have been so much a Traitour, it shall call
No other aid in your revenge: Are you
Prince Carlo?

CARLO
I was.

MARIA
That voice shall be my sentence.

[Offers to stab himself.

CARLO
Hold, I charge thee by thy honour, Manuel.

MARIA
Why did you wear this black upon you Sir?
Or how could art of man contrive a Cloud
Which this Soul had no eyes to penetrate?

CARLO
I knew thou wouldst not fight against me knowingly,
And if I fell, I meant it to secure
Thy act from punishment, when in this darkness
I took my leave o'th' World, only that boy,
Whom I compel'd to feign me wounded, so
To make thee draw thy sword; but with my blood
I feel my spirits vanish, if I have
But breath enough, I send by thee a kiss
To thy own Clara now.

MARIA
Oh, help good boy!
For 'tis no time to curse thee now, my horse
Is not far off, this scarf may stay his bleeding
Untill we meet with better Surgerie.
Now Heaven reprieve my strength but to convey him
To some good place, and I resign my self
To all the justice you will call me to.

[Exit **MANUEL** and **CELIO** carrying off **CARLO**.

SCENE III

An Apartment in the Palace.

[Enter **KING, MENDOZA, RODERIGO, ANTONIO, PEDRO, LORD.**

KING
Y'are all but my tormentors; where's Piraecquo?

[Enter **PIRACQUO.**

RODERIGO
His son is absent too.

PIRACQUOR
Have comfort Sir.

ANTONIO
Our neglect is lost in the General Cause,

What do you think my Lord Mendoza?

MENDOZA
This no news of the Prince is not so comfortable.

[Enter **1st LORD**.

KING
The news you bring?

LORD
Unless he had left the Kingdom—

KING
Be dumb—and he had left the World
Your cares might have persued him; if he
Return not, you have murdred him.

RODERIGO
My Stars are now
At work in Heaven, their influence is powerful,
I will adore the Sun if it dissolve not
This mist in which the Prince is lost; I am
Content thou be a Constellation Carlo,
In any Sphere but this.

[Enter a **MESSENGER** with a Letter to Piracquo.

PIRACQUO
To me? 'tis Manuel's character.

LORD
Unless we hear some good news of the Prince,
I fear we lose the King too.

ANTONIO
'Tis strange none should attend him but his Page.

RODERIGO
I fear some plot is practis'd 'gainst his life,
But dare not speak.

2ND LORD
That's it distracts the King,
Whose fears are helpt by a sad dream he had
Last night.

RODERIGO

My Lord Piracquo's son is missing too.

PIRACQUO
Comfort your self till my return,
I'll find 'em, or ne'r see your face agen.

KING
Well said Piracquo, all my prayers go with thee.

[Exit **PIRACQUO** and **MESSENGER**.

MENDOZA
Pedro.

PEDRO
My Lord.

MENDOZA
I know not what to say, but stand
Before, they may not see me weep.

PEDRO
Sir, I must confess—

MENDOZA
Ha! Confess?

PEDRO
You are still suspicious, have a true heart,
And let your conscience look less abroad Sir,
If he be dead, your trouble's over Sir;
We must all dye, Death has his severall waies
And times to take us off, some expire humbly
I'th' Cradle, some dismist upon a Scaffold—

[Enter **ISABELLA, MARIA, CLARA**.

MENDOZA
Come hither [takes **PEDRO** aside] doe not name a Scaffold, I
Was innocent thou knowst, the plot was all
My Ladies, and not one survives the Secret,
But we two.

PEDRO
Keep your own counsel Sir,
This Fatherly affection may doe harm,
He could not dye in better time,

KING
Madam, can you,
Whose honour seems to suffer by this absence,
Have so much charity to comfort me?

ISABELLA
He is not desperate, while we have hope.
My Lord Piracquo's son may wait upon him.

[Enter **MANUEL**.

ANTONIO
Don Manuel.

KING
Hast brought news of my Son?

MANUEL
I can inform you a sad story Sir.

ISABELLA
Where is the Prince?

MARIA
Not dead I hope.

KING
Hast thou a jealousie will concern that fear?
My soul has been a Prophet: what misfortune?

MANUEL
If you have strength to hear a truth
So sad, he has been wounded.

[Exit **ISABELLA** and **LADIES**.

KING
By what Traitour? look to the Princess.

MANUEL
I had not with such boldness undertook
The Tragick Story, if I had not brought
The great Offender.

KING
Oh, welcome Manuel—where's the Body?

MANUEL

Where it doth want no Surgery, but my Father
Is gone with all the wings his fear and duty
Can aid him with, at his return to acquaint you
With Carlo's life, or death.

RODERIGO
Would I were his Surgeon.

KING
Thou hast not nam'd the Villain yet, he may
Escape.

MANUEL
I have took order for his stay,
Untill your anger and the Laws conclude him.

KING
Thou hast done us service.

MANUEL
And it will sink by slow degrees into
Your faith, that he, who gave him all his wounds,
Was one that lov'd him faithfully.

ANTONIO
Lov'd him?

MANUEL
Above his own life.

RODERIGO
Torments oretake the Traitour.

MANUEL
'Tis not well said, with pardon of the King;
When I shall bring you to the weeping heart
Of this poor man, some may allow his penitence,
So great, it may invite a mercy to him;
Alas, he was betray'd to the black deed,
Both sword and soul compell'd to't.

KING
Here's a prodigie!

RODERIGO
Are you acquainted with the guilty person,
That you dare thus extenuate his fact?

MANUEL
I am, and dare produce him—here he stands,
So far from wishes to out-live the Prince,
He begs to wait upon his Shade.

ANTONIO
Does he not bleed?

KING
Apprehend his person.

MANUEL
They are but churlish drops,
And know not their own happiness; this wound
Was made by Carlo, yet how slow it weeps
To answer his effusion? could I reach
Their orifice, I'd kiss the crimson lips,
For his dear name that made 'em.

MANUEL
Did he kill him?
Justice Sir, Justice. I beg for Justice
Upon this Murderer.

PEDRO
Now it works.

KING
You? by what nearer interest in Carlo
Should you imagine we are slow to punish him?
'Twas a black hour when Carlo saw thee first,
Rewarded now for all his love; to prison with him,
And let him see no day.

[Exit guarded.

MARIA
I kiss your Sentence.

ANTONIO
This circumstance is strange, I am not satisfied.

[Exit **ANTONIO** after **MANUEL**.

[Enter **CLARA**.

KING
How is the Princess?

CLARA
Sir she is alive,
And would be glad to hear the Prince were so.

KING
We cannot promise, Clara. Roderigo,
We should be satisfied where his Body is,
For'tis without a Soul, I fear, by this time.

RODERIGO
I could instruct the Surgeon a way
To make that sure.

MENDOZA [To **CLARA**]
And Manuel hath confess'd himself the Murderer.

PEDRO
This change was unexpected.

CLARA
Is he gone to Prison then?

MENDOZA
Go home, by that time thou
Hast wept out all thy tears, I'll come, and tell thee
A little sad tale Clara, that shall make
An end, and we will break our hearts together.

KING
Mendoza?

MENDOZA
Sir.

KING
Why does thy grief appear
So rude to out-swell mine? he was my Son.

MENDOZA
My tears are anger Sir, as well as grief,
That he that did commit this Paricide,
Should be so impudent to say he lov'd him.

KING
That amazes me.

MENDOZA

But Traitours have their Gloss,
And dare expound their disobedient acts,
A branch of their allegiance: precious juggling
Treason would be too ugly to appear
With his own face, but Duty and Religion
Are hansome visors to abuse weak sight,
That cannot penetrate beyond the bark,
And false complexion of things; I hope
You wo'not think a single death sufficient,
If Julio dye.

KING
Carlo thou meanst—

MENDOZA
I, I, the Prince, I know not what I say Sir,
Things make me wild—

PEDRO
Take heed Sir what you say.

[Enter **ANTONIO**, **RODERIGO** at one door, and at the other door **PIRACQUO**, and a **LORD** discouraging.
PIRACQUO is return'd.

PIRACQUO
My son confess the deed, and sent to Prison? so.

KING
Now Sir.

ANTONIO
How is the Prince, my Lord?

PIRACQUO
This was an act of his last strength, as when
A short-liv'd Taper makes a blaze, it has
Direction to your Sister Sir, and I
His last commands I fear—

[**PIRACQUO** gives **ANTONIO** a Letter.

ANTONIO [To his **SERVANT**]
For the conveyance,
Trust that to me—give this Sir to my Sister.

[Exit **LORD**.

KING

Then he is dead, Piracquo?

PIRACQUO
Not yet Sir,
But he hath such a wound will not allow
Him many minutes life, 'tis mortal Sir,
They say, and wo'not pain him past next dressing.

RODERIGO
How things succeed to my Ambition—Sir—

MENDOZA
I care not for my head, now let him take it,
'Tis but for keeping counsel.

RODERIGO
It is apparent this misfortune grew
From both their loves to Clara.

KING
Thy son, Piracquo, dies.

PIRACQUO
Great Sir, hear me.

ANTONIO
Manuel affirms he did not know the Prince
I'th' habit of a More, and that his Page
By the command of Carlo told him, that
His Master had been wounded by that More,
To engage their fight.

PIRACQUO
All this the Prince acknowledg'd.

RODERIGO
These are devices to paint Manuel's Treason.

PIRACQUO
I sooner dare believe one accent from
The Prince's breath, when his just soul was parting,
Than all your Commentaries; I am bold;
Nor can the Law, and all your anger weigh
So heavy as my curse, upon his head
That durst lift up a Sword to wound the Prince:
But let not passion take away your justice,
'Tis that I kneel for.

KING
Against whom Piracquo?

PIRACQUO
'Gainst him that's guilty of the Prince's loss,
You may incline to think poor Manuel innocent.

KING
What riddle's this?

RODERIGO
Has not your son, Piracquo,
Confess'd himself the Murderer?

ANTONIO
Manuel's fortune
Distracts the old man.

PIRACQUO
Pardon my love of truth, I here accuse
Mendoza, that hath slept so long in Treason.

MENDOZA
Ha—Pe—Pedro.

PIRACQUO
If he deny, I ha' proof to make him blush,
And sink him with dishonour; Pedro can
Relate a Story will be worth your wonder.

MENDOZA
Nay then 'tis come about, I see,
I cannot Sir confess in better time.
Don Manuel has accus'd himself unjustly
For Carlo's death, that Prince, if I may trust
A Wife upon her death-bed—

[Takes **RODERIGO** aside.

[Enter **ISABELLA**.

KING
Roderigo—
Give us account from their examination,
And guide us in this Labyrinth. Piracquo
Return toth' Prince, what Death hath left of him
Command may be attended hither.

ISABELLA
Sir, if you please, I have a great desire
To take a sad leave of the Prince, and kiss
His pale hand, ere his Body be embalm'd,
And sear-cloths hide him from us.

KING
It will but
Enlarge your grief.

ANTONIO
I will attend my Sister; my Lord Piracquo
You can best direct us.

[Exit **ANTONIO, PIRACQUO, ISABELLA**.

RODERIGO
Convey 'em with a strong guard.

[**MEN** and **PEDRO** under guard.

PEDRO
What think you of an Indian voyage now Sir?

RODERIGO
My joyes are firm at root [aside] Don Manuel,
Sir, is not guilty of the Prince's death,
Yet stain'd with blood to merit execution.
He that is slain did but usurp your blessing,
And was by the art of Duke Mendoza's Lady,
Then Governess to the Prince, after the loss
Of Carlo, that was stolen away an infant,
Put in his place; the Court has been long cosen'd.

KING
This story will want faith.

MENDOZA
The circumstance will make all clear.

KING
Expound the riddle as we walk, there's no
Condition more expos'd to care than Princes.
Private men meet the force of common stings,
But none can feel the weight of Kings, but Kings.

[Exeunt.

ACT V

SCENE I

A Cell in the Prison.

Enter **MENDOZA** and the **CASTELLANO**.

MENDOZA
A Very goodly pile; a hansom prison!

CASTELLANO
It has been grac'd with persons of some honor,

MENDOZA
They had but little grace, as well as I,
That came to be your Tenants for all that.
Signior, where is my quondam servant?
My fellow prisoner, Pedro.

CASTELLANO
He is singing, Sir.

MENDOZA
What?

CASTELLANO
Catches.

MENDOZA
He has a fine time on't.
He need not clear his throat for a confession,
He has done that already, and I too;
That trouble's over; and yet call him hither;
But I'll not sing.

[Exit **CASTELLANO**.

Poor Julio, thou art gone,
And with thy eyes all my delights are clos'd,
My senses vanish too apace—I was
Too hasty when my Duchess lay a dying
To visit her; had I but stayd one hour,
She had been speechless, and I had been happy
Without the reach of this unlucky Secret.

[Enter **CASTELLANO** and **PEDRO**.

PEDRO
Does the house fill, Sir? these are active times,
And if all men had their deserts, the State
Must be at charge to build new tenements
For Traytors.

CASTELLANO
The times are busie, Sir.

PEDRO
They are indeed,
Good for al squires of the delinquent body
And sable Twig.

CASTELLANO
You are very pleasant, Sir.

PEDRO
You would not smile, I think, so much, if Justice
Should take a toy and turn about, it is
Within the hand of fate to fetch a compass,
With your own rod, & whip, you know what follows.

[Exit **CASTELLANO**.

MENDOZA
Is this a time and place convenient, Pedro,
To sing your catches?

PEDRO
Yes, and please your Grace.
And cause my songs are set for three parts, Sir,
If it will please your Grace to take the Tenor,
And get the Prince's Page, newly committed,
To sing the Treble, for the Base, let me alone.

MENDOZA
You can sing that part at first sight.

PEDRO
I can reach double ef-fa-uth: Shall the boy come?

MENDOZA
Yes, yes, why should I grieve?

PEDRO

Why now you are right;
Let men that have no hope to get their freedom
Be fullen, whine like whelps, and break their sleep,
We must be jolly, and drink sack, and sing.

MENDOZA
We! why we? is any thing in our condition
Can promise hope to be enlarg'd before
The rest? our state, if you consider, Pedro,
Exceeds, in being desperate, other mens,
As we out-sin them in the fact.

PEDRO
Why, there's your error, we are in for Treason, Sir,
That's to our comfort.

MENDOZA
Comfort? can there be
A greater charge?

PEDRO
Oh our discharge the nearer;
Poor things, whose highest thoughts are pilfering,
Lie by't, and languish Sessions after Sessions,
Till they have worn away their clothes, and skins too,
And often are repriev'd, when he that's sent
Hitherfor Treason, quickly comes to th'bar,
Pleads his not guilty, and is hang'd compendiously.

MENDOZA
Yet some, with reverence to your observations,
Are not dispatch'd.

PEDRO
Then, doubt their causes mainly;
Your Grace, I hope, shall not complain for want
Of timely execution; I am thinking
What Speech is best to please the people at it.

MENDOZA
I shall have cause to name your treachery.

PEDRO
Why so, there's more argument by that
To stuff out your confession.

MENDOZA
Tell me, and tell me truly,

How long since you discover'd this Court Secret
To Don Piracquo?

PEDRO
I was tender hearted, Sir,
And knew that I had but a weak memory,
Therefore the first time that I saw his Lordship,
After he came from Portugal, I told him
The punctual story, lest I should forget, Sir;
What should a man dissemble, & lose time for?
I did it for your good.

MENDOZA
It does appear.

PEDRO
It was no fault of mine, you came no sooner
To this preferment.

MENDOZA
It might have sav'd my Julio's life indeed,
And then though I had died—

PEDRO
Yet you were against it still;
These jealousies and fears do seldom prosper;
I knew by instinct t' were better, but as it is
'Tis well, your death will be more pittied,
And remarkable.

MENDOZA
But what have you got by betraying me?

PEDRO
The credit to be hang'd for treason, as
I told your Grace, besides the benefit
Of being read in Chronicles with Lords,
And men of worship, I have prepar'd a business,
For the present, a provision, Sir,
Will serve any turn.

MENDOZA
What's that?

PEDRO
A ballad, Sir,
Before I die, to let the people know
How I behav'd my self upon the scaffold;

With other passages, that will delight
The people, when I take my leave of the world,
Made to a Pavin tune,
Will you hear it?

[Enter **CASTELLANO** and **CLARA**.

MENDOZA
Away you knave.

CASTELLANO
Sir, your Daughter.

[Exit.

PEDRO
She comes to condole.
I'll see you another time; your Graces servant.

[Exit.

CLARA
Sir, I beseech you tell me, for I dare not
Believe the busy noise, they say you have
Confest strange things, and he that was receiv'd
These many years, Prince Carlo, and so lately
Slain, is my brother Julio.

MENDOZA
Sad truth, Clara.

CLARA
I have heard my Mother say, he dyed an infant.

MENDOZA
And I believ'd it too, but at her death
She told me another story, Clara, that
Prince Carlo by some Pirats had been stolen
An infant from our Castle, on which loss,
She sent me word to Court, my son died suddenly;
At which the King fearing some danger might
Follow to the Prince her charge, commanded him
To court, instead of whom, she sent thy brother,
Who was believ'd the Kingdoms heir, until
Pedro, who waited then nearest thy Mother,
And knew the imposture, brake his oath, and told
Piracquo all the Secret, by whose charge
My death and shame must make up the full Tragedy.

CLARA
Manuel kill'd my brother then?

MENDOZA
He has don't;
And if thou hast a Sister's soul, thou must
Join with thy father, to pull curses on him.

CLARA
That will not call poor Julio back again;
They say that Charity will open Heaven.

MENDOZA
Charity? will you not curse your brother's murderer?
Upon my blessing I command thee curse him.

CLARA
That would but wound us more, & not reach him;
Beside, 'twere an intrenchment upon heaven,
So boldly to prescribe our own revenge,
It were a sin might draw another punishment,
Great as the loss of you.

MENDOZA
You are a baggage;
But if thou hast a thought to wish him live,
Here I disclame thee; if thou wert a son,
I would pronounce thee bastard, if thou didst not
Kill himself thy self, but as it is, I sha'not
Be satisfied, since my own hands are bound,
If thou attempt not something in his danger.

CLARA
Good Sir, you speak, as you were to expect
No killing sentence from the offended Law.

MENDOZA
I'll study some revenge my self.

[Exit:

CLARA
He's lost;
And in this storm like a distracted passenger,
Whose bark has struck upon some sand, I look
From the forsaken deck upon the seas,
I find my own despair, which every wave

Swels high, and bids me die for fear of drowning.

[Enter **CASTELLANO**.

May I not see Don Manuel your prisoner?

CASTELLANO
Yes Madam, if you expect until
Princess Maria, who is come to visit him—

CLARA
My affairs concern 'em both,
Direct me with more hast.

CASTELLANO
Then this way, Madam.

[Exeunt

SCENE II

Another Cell of the same. A Taper on the Table.

[Enter **MANUEL** and **MARIA**.

MARIA
Madam, I ow to your charity this light,
And yet this little Taper may be useless,
I fear the King will lose part of his sentence
When you go hence, for such a full light waits
About you, when you take away your person,
It will be some day still, as I foresee
As you appear'd some dawning of the morning.

MARIA
I would I could bring comfort to thee, Manuel!

MANUEL
What comfort can you wish me?

MARIA
Life and liberty;
With these my self, if fate, and thy consent
Were to allow the gift.

MANUEL

It is not well,
Unless you doubted, Madam, my repentance,
To afflict me with these mockeries.
When will you rather perfect what your own
Revenge must prompt you to, my death for Carlo,
Your Princely Brother, Madam? I confess
This hand rob'd him of life.

MARIA
Yet in my heart
I dare pronounce thy pardon, Manuel.

MANUEL
It is not possible.

[Enter **CLARA**.

Is not that Clara?
That's come to take her leave, before I print
My everlasting farewell on her lip?
Which I shall hardly find, if this rain last,
To drown these lovely meadows; thou shalt be
A Judge between the Princess and poor Manuel,
To enable thee for sentence, take upon thee
Her person, Clara; Be the Princess, wo't?
And hear me plead against my self and her,
Till she repent her love, and leave me to
A quiet death. I know not how to think
(Maria) you can mean this love to me,
Or that your voice, when it does chime the sweetest,
Is more than preface to my dirge; say that
You have a heart less penetrable than
The scale of Dragons, and as many stings
When they make war, and I'll give faith to you;
For such an enemy as I, must not
Be look'd on, but with all your wrath upon me;
Me-thinks I hear your brother call you, Madam,
And hovering, as he scorn'd to touch the earth
Sustains his Murderer, is pointing to
The wounds I made, whose fountains are still weeping.
I feel a purple dew descend upon me,
And I am all a bloody rock already;
Are not you stiff with wonder yet? if once
You had when I appear'd a man, fair thoughts
Of me; it is too much to love me now,
You must convert them into curses, Madam,
And I will call it justice.

CLARA

I came not
To hear this Comment on my brother's story,
Whom you have kill'd.

MANUEL

Observe her act your person,
And speak now, as if the sorrow were her own,
And she had lost a brother.

CLARA

Indeed,
I have wept before, and came not now to learn
A grief for him that was so near my blood:
But I've consider'd too, the ties of nature
Should have no force against the rules of Justice;
Although it be a sorrow, to remember
He took his great misfortune from your sword,
You did not murder him, nay you did not kill him,
You fought in his revenge, and while he came
Hid in the name and person of a Traytor,
It was your virtue made him bleed, and yet
He was my brother, Sir.

MANUEL

Your brother? more,
He was your Prince too, Madam, think o' that,
The full blown expectation of the Kingdom,
One that redeem'd my life from banishment,
And yet I kill'd him, can you forgive me?
You cannot, must not, Madam.

CLARA

Yes, and dare
Say, I still love you.

MANUEL

She will punish me,
For giving up my interest to Carlo,
If she encourage thus Maria, Madam,
Do you consider how few sands are left
In my poor glass of time, I cannot promise
Three minutes here, Law and the Kings decree
Have turn'd two parts of me to dust already;
I feel the third unsettle, and make fit
To be dissolv'd, but could fate give my life
The period to be wished (remember whom
I speak to Clara) and I need no more

Accuse my self, my heart was long since given
Away, and you as soon may reconcile
Time and Eternity to one growth, and age,
As hope my love and yours should ever meet.

CLARA
Then it is time to dye.

MANUEL
Madam, she faints,
Oh help, she has forgot her part, this was
Not meant to Clara.

MARIA
Madam, Madam.

MANUEL
Clara, so, so, she returns,
I should have quickly followed else.

MARIA
I see
Your loves are sacred, and 'tis sin to attempt
Your separation; though I lov'd thee Manuel,
I can resign to Clara, whom I hop'd
Her Brothers death might have provok'd to leave thee.

MANUEL
Her Brothers? let me hear Clara speak; her Brothers death?
Having so little time to stay with thee
Alive, why didst thou make such hast?

CLARA
Did not
You Sir pronounce it was impossible
That our two loves should meet?

MANUEL
Thou didst not
Represent Clara then, thou wert the Princess.

CLARA
I know not, but your last profession
That our two hearts should never grow together,
Followed so close my Brother's death, I thought
The meaning look'd on me.

MARIA

Thy Brothers death?

MARIA
You have not slain the Prince my Brother, Manuel,
But Clara's, this may yet appear a mystery.

CLARA
'Tis too true.

MANUEL
But stay; and can my Clara then forgive me?
No man despair to find Mercy in Heaven,
There is so great a Charity upon Earth.
But doe not leave me lost i'th' wonder, Madam,
Although it would be happiness to know
The Prince not dead, I cannot hear without
A wound next his, that I ha' kil'd thy Brother;
It cannot be, although thou wouldst forgive me,
I cannot be so miserable.

MARIA
How
Their Souls agree? 'twere tyranny to part 'em.
Clara, I envyed, now allow thy happiness,
And will have no more thoughts upon your loves,
But what shall be employ'd in hearty wishes
That Manuel may live still to reward it;
Thou hast deserv'd him better than I have
Antonio.

CLARA
If my death may speak
Addition to the love I owe thee; 'tis
In my resolution, at that minute
Thy Soul takes leave, my own shall wait upon it,
And take a journey through the Clouds together:
Who knows but they may fill one Star? Farewell,
Till we begin that progress.

MANUEL
Doe not make
Death horrid to me Clara, for to think,
When this unworthy Frame must fall to pieces,
Thy Soul, a fairer Tenant to this building,
Should wander in pursuit of mine—

MARIA
No more;

Let me advise your griefs, I have tears for both,
Divide at distance, you may kiss in heart.

MANUEL
With such a groan souls from their body parts

[The **CASTELLANO** lights away the **LADIES**, and **MANUEL** retires to his Prison.

SCENE III

An Apartment in the Palace.

[Enter **RODERIGO** and **ISABELLA**.

ISABELLA
How, an Impostor! though the Peoples tongues,
That catch at every noise, and wave their duty,
As they are prescrib'd by Faction, or lewd Pamphlets,
Doe talk this loud—

RODERIGO
Upon my honour, Madam.

ISABELLA
I hope your Lordship has another knowledge,
And faith, than to disgrace your blood, the Prince—

RODERIGO
I say he is no Prince, and we are sorry
A Lady of your greatness should i'th' height
Of such a glorious expectation, lose
What did invite your person hither.

ISABELLA
Ha!
Then I am lost, that Letter has undone me,
Which full of love and satisfaction, made
Me hasty to destroy my self.

RODERIGO
'Tis yet
Within your choice to lose no honour, Madam,
And in my sense of what you else might suffer,
I come to tender reparation,
Both to your love and greatness.

ISABELLA

'Tis not possible.

RODERIGO

If you can find within your heart a will
To entertain my love, I'm no Impostor,
The King will call me Brother, be kind Madam,
And what is past shall vanish like a dream.
Secure me with a smile.

ISABELLA

My Lord, I thank you;
But there will still remain some characters
By which the world may guess at my sad story.

RODERIGO

There cannot.

ISABELLA

Yes, I find some printed here,
For I did love the person, I confess,
Of him you call the Impostor: did he know
Himself a Counterfeit?

RODERIGO

Let me be just,
And quit him from that Treason.

ISABELLA

That is something
To plead his innocence to me; I dare not
Yet ask his name, when I remember what
My tongue consented to before the Priest
So late; yet 'twill be known; if he be not
The Prince we thought, tel me his other name;
Say, is he basely born?

RODERIGO

He is the Duke
Mendoza's son.

ISABELLA

That is a comfort yet,
And in the confidence of this truth, my Lord,
I am well again, I thank you.

RODERIGO

If this please you,

Doe you remember Madam, he hath wounds
Fatal upon him, that already may
Exclude him from the living?

ISABELLA
'T would be impious,
While there is any life remaining Sir,
To make another promise; when you say
He's dead, I may with modest freedom hear
What you too early now prepare me for.

[Exit **ISABELLA**

RODERIGO
You honour me enough.
I find her judgement
Already meet what I propound, he cannot,
He sha'not live to cross me.

[Enter **PIRACQUO**.

'Tis Piracquo,
He can assure me; you look sad my Lord,
As if with Julio's giving up the ghost,
Your sons life now were forfeit.

PIRACQUO
'Tis too true.

RODERIGO
I'll follow, and acquaint her; yet 'tis safer
She take it from another.

PIRACQUO
All my hopes
Are in your Grace, the King is coming hither,
If you will bind an old mans prayers, and service,
Second my feeble breath, and mediate
His mercy to my boy, you may be satisfied
In conscience, he had no thoughts to kill him;
The Prince's death will not engage you now
To be poor Manuel's enemy; good my Lord,
Forgive what past in my rash language.

RODERIGO
Does not
Your Lordship call to mind there was a sum
Of fifty thousand Ducats?

PIRACQUO

They shall be sent to your Grace's Secretary, nay
I'll make 'em fifty thousand more, and think
It cheap to save his life, now you are merciful—

RODERIGO

The bargain would doe well, but you are cozen'd,
I will not take a Maravidi, not I,
If upon other honourable tearms
I may possess you favour, I shall meet
Your just commands; ha' you forgot my Lord?
Some men doe keep Records, but I am charitable,
And will not rack your patience—

PIRACQUO

Y'are gratious.

RODERIGO

Ten millions of Ducats shall not ransom
Your Darling from the Scaffold: you observe?
You know your self, your fortune, and upon
What strength you must depend, now I have said—

PIRACQUO

Will your Grace hear?
My son shall live then, and not lose one hair,
If you would pawn your soul to have it otherwise.
I have said too.

RODERIGO

So peremptory?

PIRACQUO

Your Grace must pardon me the truth, I have
A scurvy sullen humour where I meet
A worse, and cannot hold, though I should hang for't,
And so God bu'y to your Grace, we are alone—

RODERIGO

Be merry with your head on—time may come—

PIRACQUO

I would take boldness, once more, to intreat
That the young man may live till the next Spring,
And then your Grace may purge—

RODERIGO

So Sir,
I shall find ways to stay your vomiting—
The King.

[Enter **KING** and **LORDS**.

1ST LORD
Good Sir be comforted.

KING
Good Sir give me reasons;
I had a son till now, yet long since lost him.

RODERIGO
Now you may take revenge.

KING
Tis well remembred.
Mendoza is the Traytor, he shall bleed
For Carlo's loss.

RODERIGO
And he deserves, that would
Have cozen'd the whole Kingdom.

KING
Send for him;
I'll ask him in what wilderness the boy
Has hid himself, command him hither presently,
And if he give me not a satisfaction,
It will be justice then to send his soul
About the world, to find him out.

1ST LORD
The Prince Antonio, Sir.

[Enter **ANTONIO** and **MARIA**.

ANTONIO
If at a time, when sorrow
Hath exercised his sting, you can admit
To hear me happy in Maria's love,
Let me begin to call you father, and
Till Carlo find your blessing, think you have
One to supply his duty.

KING
It is some

Allay to Carlo's loss, Maria has
Not left her father.

MARIA
I shall ever live
Within your precept to express a daughter
As unto him a wife.

KING
Both to my heart!
Sit down, where is your sister Isabella?

RODERIGO
She not despairs
To be a Bride to one, that may repair
My Nephews loss; and if she smile on me,
It wil not draw I hope your frown upon it.

[Enter **ISABELLA**, **JULIO** and **PIRACQUO**.

ANTONIO
Is not that Isabella?

ISABELLA
And this he,
Who, if you call me Sister, must be worth
Your noblest Friendship, and embrace.

RODERIGO
Alive?

JULIO
Your pardon Sir, they knew me innocent,
Made me usurp Prince Carlo's name for Julio's.

RODERIGO
Confusion!

[Enter **MANUEL** and **CLARA**.

PIRACQUO
I appeal Sir to your justice, and have brought
My son, to hear your breath pronounce his pardon.

KING
Thus all meet happiness but I; receive
Him free Piracquo, only I must mourn
The loss of mine.

[Enter **MENDOZA** and **PEDRO**.

JULIO
I am no Prince, Don Manuel, my fate
Has been unriddled.

CLARA
My Brother living? we are all safe.

MENDOZA
Ha, my Julio?

JULIO
Your blessing now.

MENDOZA
Take it, and with it all my tears, I scorn
To shed one other drop, my joyes are mighty,
My heart is all one bonefire—

KING
Plead no more,
Mendoza dies, the sentence is irrevocable.

PEDRO
There is a cooler Sir after your bonefire.

JULIO
Sister, I'll kiss these sorrows off.

CLARA
You cannot while my Father's doom'd to death.

RODERIGO
Why does Mendoza live?

PIRACQUO
Because he must not dye yet. Pedro—

PEDRO
My Lord.

[**PIRACQUO** and **PEDRO** whisper with the **KING**.

MENDOZA
I'll give thee Clara first, here take her Manuel,
I see she loves thee, lose no tears for me,

My Taper has burnt dim this many years.

KING
Antonio! Maria! Isabella!
Mendoza! witness all—proceed Piracquo—

PIRACQUO
I was that Pirate Sir, that stole your son,
And being desperate meant by this surprise
To make my peace—

PEDRO
I was in the Confederacy,
And must affirm this truth.

PIRACQUO
But just when I had fitted my design,
And did expect t' have brought Don Carlo home,
I heard he was at Court, no loss deplor'd,
For by the Duchess of Mendoza's art
Julio supply'd the Princes name, and person.

MENDOZA
And sent me word to Court my Son was dead? ha!

PIRACQUO
This made me think my Kinsman had deceiv'd me,
And then resolv'd my stay in Portugal,
Where, as my own, I bred, and call'd him Manuel;
Till after many years your Grace redeem'd us,
And I at my return confirm'd i'th' story
By Pedro, hitherto protracted time,
With hope to serve Don Julio for our freedome.
I have your pardon Sir for all.

KING
Thou hast.

PEDRO
I am included, trust me with a Secret Sir
Another time, I knew 't would come to this
At last, and with some justice did but punish
Your fears and jealousies; is not this better
Than sending me to the Wars, or shipping me
For t' other World before my time?

MENDOZA
Th'art my best Servant.

PIRACQUO
And my heir agen.

CARLO
Depose me from this glorious title, Sir,
Unless my Clara may divide the honor.

KING
Providence meant her thine, both call me father.

RODERIGO
There is no remedy, Nephew, welcome home,
And Niece, we shall be kindred now Mendoza,
Piracquo we are friends too, and I'll try,
How I can love you heartily.

KING
I hear
The Altar call, make hast, the triumph will
Attend too long, the clouds are chac'd away,
Night ne'r was mother to so bright a day.

[Exeunt **OMNES**.

FINIS.

JAMES SHIRLEY – A CONCISE BIBLIOGRAPHY

The following includes years of first publication, and of performance if known, together with dates of licensing by the Master of the Revels if available.

TRAGEDIES
The Maid's Revenge (licensed 9th February 1626; printed, 1639)
The Traitor (licensed 4th May 1631; printed, 1635)
Love's Cruelty (licensed 14th November 1631; printed, 1640)
The Politician (acted, 1639; printed, 1655)
The Cardinal (licensed 25th May 1641; printed, 1652).

TRAGI-COMEDIES
The Grateful Servant (licensed 3rd November 1629 as The Faithful Servant; printed 1630)
The Young Admiral (licensed 3rd July 1633; printed 1637)
The Coronation (licensed 6th February 1635, as Shirley's, but printed in 1640 as a work of John Fletcher)
The Duke's Mistress (licensed 18th January 1636; printed 1638)
The Gentleman of Venice (licensed 30th October 1639; printed 1655)
The Doubtful Heir (printed 1652), licensed as Rosania, or Love's Victory in 1640

The Imposture (licensed 10th November 1640; printed 1652)
The Court Secret (printed 1653).

COMEDIES
Love Tricks, or the School of Complement (licensed 10th February 1625; printed under its subtitle, 1631)
The Wedding (ca. 1626; printed 1629)
The Brothers (licensed 4th November 1626; printed 1652)
The Witty Fair One (licensed 3rd October 1628; printed 1633)
The Humorous Courtier (licensed 17th May 1631; printed 1640).
The Changes, or Love in a Maze (licensed 10th January 1632; printed 1639)
Hyde Park (licensed 20th April 1632; printed 1637)
The Ball (licensed 16th November 1632; printed 1639)
The Bird in a Cage, or The Beauties (licensed 21st January 1633; printed 1633)
The Gamester (licensed 11th November 1633; printed 1637)
The Example (licensed 24th June 1634; printed 1637)
The Opportunity (licensed 29th November 1634; printed 1640)
The Lady of Pleasure (licensed 15th October 1635; printed 1637)
The Royal Master (acted and printed 1638)
The Constant Maid, or Love Will Find Out the Way (printed 1640)
The Sisters (licensed 26th April 1642; printed 1653).
Honoria and Mammon (printed 1659)

DRAMAS
A Contention for Honor and Riches (printed 1633), morality play
The Triumph of Peace (licensed 3rd February 1634; printed 1634), masque
The Arcadia (printed 1640), pastoral tragicomedy
St. Patrick for Ireland (printed 1640), neo-miracle play
The Triumph of Beauty (ca. 1640; printed 1646), masque
The Contention of Ajax and Ulysses (printed 1659), entertainment
Cupid and Death (performed 26th March 1653; printed 1659), masque

www.ingramcontent.com/pod-product-compliance
Lightning Source LLC
Chambersburg PA
CBHW070108070426
42448CB00038B/2035